D1433791

THE
SILENT
HOUSES
OF BRITAIN

Virginia creeper almost obscuring the façade of Edwinsford House

THE SILENT HOUSES OF BRITAIN

ALEXANDER CRESWELL

Macdonald Illustrated

To my late father, Sir Michael Creswell
who taught me to search for The Spirit of Place

A **Macdonald Illustrated** BOOK

© Alexander Creswell 1991

First published in Great Britain in 1991 by Macdonald & Co (Publishers) Ltd, London and Sydney
A member of Maxwell Macmillan Pergamon Publishing Coporation

All rights reserved
No part of this publication may be reproduced, stored in a retrieval system, or transmitted, in any form or by any means without the prior permission of the publisher, nor be otherwise circulated in any form of binding or cover other than that in which it is published and without a similar condition including this condition being imposed on the subsequent purchaser.

British Library Cataloguing in Publication Data
Creswell, Alexander
   The Silent Houses of Britain.
   1. England. Empty houses
   1. Title
   307, 336

   ISBN 0–356–19680–1

Typeset by Wyvern Typesetting Ltd
Printed and bound in Hong Kong. Produced by Mandarin

Publisher: Celia Kent
Editor: John Wainwright
Designer: John Heritage
Production Controller: Caroline Bennett

Macdonald and Co (Publishers) Ltd
Orbit House
1 New Fetter Lane
London EC4A 1AR

ACKNOWLEDGEMENTS

My thanks to all who have helped and encouraged me throughout the development of this book. In particular I am indebted to 'SAVE Britain's Heritage' and Marcus Binney, who provided the initial inspiration, to Lord Bute and 'Recollections', who invested a great deal of faith and time into keeping the impetus going, and to Anthony Spink for seeing the potential for an exhibition at the end of it.

For their help with research, I am grateful to Caroline Grayburn and Dana Dean. For all the draft reading and thumbing through dictionaries, I thank Simon Westcott and my mother, Lady Creswell. Most of all, I thank Mary Green for her constant encouragement, for her tremendous ability to organise, and for her companionship as I dragged her around the kingdom to share this passion of mine.

Alexander Creswell

"There must be many people . . . whose good sense could surely be touched if it were clearly put to them that they were destroying what they, or more surely still, their sons and son's sons, would one day fervently long for, and which no wealth or energy could ever buy again for them."

William Morris
'Anti-Scrape'
The Athenaeum – 10th March 1877

CONTENTS

EXPLANATION 9

HISTORICAL NOTE 11

INTRODUCTION BY MARCUS BINNEY, O.B.E. 15

CAVEAT 21

HIGHCLIFFE CASTLE 23

ASHMANS HALL 27

MINTO HOUSE 31

HIGH HEAD CASTLE 33

COPPED HALL 35

BUCHANAN CASTLE 39

CARADOC COURT 41

KIRKLINTON HALL 45

GUY'S CLIFFE 47

DUNMORE HOUSE 51

WITLEY COURT 53

ABERGLASNEY 57

EDWINSFORD HOUSE 61

STOCKEN HALL 63

OULTON HALL 65

REVESBY ABBEY 67

POLTALLOCH HOUSE 71

ECTON HALL 75

MAVISBANK HOUSE 77

PENICUIK HOUSE 81

PELL WALL HALL   85

PIERCEFIELD HOUSE   89

BETTISFIELD PARK   91

BANK HALL   95

GWYLFA HIRAETHOG   99

MELTON CONSTABLE   101

ECCLESGRIEG HOUSE   103

URIE HOUSE   105

BELLADRUM HOUSE   109

LOUDON CASTLE   111

VALE ROYAL ABBEY   113

RUPERRA CASTLE   115

PICKHILL HALL   119

BUNTINGSDALE HALL   121

SINAI PARK   125

ABERPERGWM HOUSE   127

WOODCHESTER PARK   129

GIBSIDE   133

CAMS HALL   135

HOUSE OF GRAY   139

WARDHOUSE   141

BARON HILL   143

YEATON PEVERY   147

CRAWFORD PRIORY   149

SUMMERFOLD HOUSE   151

SOURCES AND FURTHER READING   152

LIST OF ILLUSTRATIONS   154

INDEX   158

ENDPIECE   160

The façade of the house was once used for target practice, Piercefield

The garden gates swung open, Caradoc Court – a detail

EXPLANATION

" If he wants to paint a silent house, why doesn't he come and paint ours – nobody says a word there", joked a man recently, during one of those 'what-do-*you*-do' conversations. During the five years that I have been involved in compiling this book, I have been repeatedly asked to explain the term 'silent' houses.

"Oh, you mean *ruined* houses . . .", continues the probing. No, not exactly; a ruin exists as a ruin, and will probably remain as such – albeit with mown grass, tidy edges and small signs dotted about as in a museum. Traditionally ruins are synonymous with romance; from the ivy-clad remains of ancient Rome to the manicured order of Fountains Abbey they have inspired writers and artists for centuries. However, ruins are often passive and preserved, their spirit subordinate to the guide-book and their silence broken by the clicking of cameras.

"Well, *derelict* then . . ." Derelict is an ugly word, implying something sinister and distasteful. At the mention of it the subject of the conversation changes. Yet, while many of these houses could be described as derelict, instead of repugnance I found a unique atmosphere in their abandoned shells – intangible, invisible and above all, silent.

Somewhere between the lost romanticism of ruination and the unfaithful neglect of dereliction lies the essence of this silence; these houses were once inhabited, and most will be again, but like the interval in a play when the curtain is down, they have been temporarily abandoned. Moreover, Nature flourishes where Man's indifference allows it – the rain gets in, the roof collapses, trees grow within, and gradually the house recedes into its natural surroundings. But then one day the builders move in and restoration begins. The house comes alive again – the atmosphere of decay succeeded by the smell of fresh paint.

So, I have simply interpreted what I have seen; provided an individual glimpse of a house at one moment in its history. This is neither a call to arms nor a morbid celebration of decline; neither a study in sentimentality nor an incitement to trespass. In putting this collection of paintings together I did and do not try to pass judgement on either the houses or their owners, nor do I attempt to champion a cause. In my paintings I look beyond the indifference of decay to find the spirit in the Silent Houses of Britain.

Looking into the stair hall, Oulton Hall – a detail

Three storeys of stairs, Cams Hall – a detail

HISTORICAL NOTE

The end of the Industrial Revolution marked the beginning of the decline of the Country House in Britain. The power and fortunes of the important families who had run the country until then grew from the fact that they owned a vast acreage of land, which produced money, and therefore power. Association with other great families, through social and marital intercourse, only served to increase that power. Often the estates of two families were merged by marriage into a single and more powerful union, at whose head was, more often than not, an influential member of Parliament. Once established there was very little to hinder the progress of such a family, in commerce or government.

The Country House was not only a home and base, but also a demonstration of power; it being designed to impress, especially those whose position could pose a threat to the status and prosperity of its occupants. The size and style of the house, the extravagance of the interior and the flamboyance of the lifestyle it played host to, all indicated the ambition of the owner. As a family grew in stature, so their house was enlarged or even completely rebuilt. Sometimes such expansion had the unfortunate effect of tipping the balance and bankrupting the owner, his ambitions having outpaced his means.

Regardless of the misfortunes of the few, the trend continued towards more extravagant houses up until the middle years of the Industrial Revolution. However the changes in society during the Revolution brought about an eventual decline. Britain had been a wholly rural economy, but with the advent of the power of industry that wealth was duplicated. The successful industrialist needed to integrate with the aristocracy, and did so by building himself a great house that gave him the passport to that integration – namely, marriage. After one or two generations, integration was virtually complete and wealth continued to grow. Yet at the same time the traditional power was becoming diluted. The Reform Acts of 1832 and 1867, and the Ballot Act of 1872, reorganized the system of boroughs and voting that had given the land-owner a monopoly in local power. Thus by 1875 the landowner had become a minority in the House of Commons and, soon after, on the Justices' bench as well, while the new County Councils of 1888 deprived him of power even in his home area.

A stone fountain, Caradoc Court

The stairs at Urie House – a colour note

The agricultural depression of the mid-1870s exacerbated this dilution of power. Agricultural development on a vast scale in the American Mid-West, and the ease of trade with the New World combined to make the working of land in Britain less profitable. By the turn of the century this particular shake-down had had its effect; many land-owners being forced to sell off their land and, in some extreme cases, the house too. However, wiser families had already put their eggs into several commercial and industrial baskets; their sons were sent into the City, into the hitherto unacceptable world of trade, and were encouraged to marry into the family of a wealthy industrialist.

By the turn of the century this process of reversion and integration was complete, and for a while the Country House enjoyed an Indian Summer, but its purpose had changed. No longer was the country seat a power-base, but merely a residence in the country; no longer would it put its owner in the running for Parliament, but it did give him the luxury of a beautiful place in which to relax and entertain, free of the encumbrance of office or factory. Thus existed the society of perpetual sunshine and cucumber sandwiches which P.G. Wodehouse was to describe in such vivid and delightful detail.

Gradually, however, the clouds gathered over the late Victorian age. While Britain's supremacy in the world of industry became overshadowed by greater production in America and, later, in Germany, unprecedented wealth and the disparity with the condition of the working classes sent a quiver through the foundations of society. Marx and Engels attacked Capitalism and social reformers sought to improve the lot of the downtrodden worker. In 1870 the State intervened with the Education Act, which provided universal elementary education. New laws were introduced in Parliament and the great families were now powerless to stop them. The coup-de-grâce came with the introduction of death-duties in 1894, an unprecedented tourniquet on the wealthier families, old and new alike.

By the end of the First World War it became obvious that the heyday was over. Throughout society many families had lost their men – fathers, sons, uncles and cousins – and the ensuing death-duties crippled those who survived. Many of those who had worked in the great houses were now unwilling to return to service, preferring to work in offices or factories, which offered better hours, better pay and more independence. Thus for the wealthy the future became very bleak indeed. In less than half a generation, many households faced the end of the healthy prosperity created by their forebears.

To many families it was impossible to carry on in unhappy isolation, and they sold off their estates. Of those put up for sale, the land was snapped up by the tenants, but the mansions were unwanted. Deprived of the land that supported them they were unlikely ever to be lived in again. Gradually contents were sold off in sad auctions on the front lawns. Furniture and chattels were cast to the four winds, the treasures of generations of collectors and aesthetes broken up and scattered, often for pitifully low prices. And whatever was kept was often chopped up or cut down – great tables were sawn in half to fit into the smaller dower house, for example.

Those families that survived the devastation of the First World War faced a further disaster during the Second – namely, requisitioning by the armed forces. After the War many houses were returned to their owners in a state beyond repair. Thus in the 1950s the market was flooded with great houses in increasingly poor condition, and few buyers could be found, other than the vultures – demolition men and builders interested only in the raw materials. In all some 600 houses were destroyed, while others became corporately owned as business headquarters and training centres, and some became state-owned hospitals and institutions.

So great houses disappeared, out of sight and out of mind, and it was not until a whole new generation began to realise what was happening that efforts were made to slow the destruction. At the end of the War, the Gowers report had stated that the government *must* offer incentive and relief to those fortunate, or unfortunate enough to own historic houses. Yet by 1974 many of the recommendations in the report were still unfulfilled, and the destruction was continuing. The problem of awareness as to the extent of the damage was of paramount importance, and an energetic triumvirate of architectural experts – Roy Strong, John Harris and Marcus Binney – compiled a survey of houses that had been destroyed. They presented their findings in a startling exhibition at the Victoria and Albert Museum; 'The Destruction of the Country House' offered a gruesome display of loss to the world.

From the exhibition was born SAVE Britain's Heritage, a charitable foundation dedicated to the defence of the houses themselves. Marcus Binney, its founder, believed that while putting pressure on the government on the one hand, owners should on the other hand be strongly dissuaded from shrugging their responsibilities. In the case of Barlaston Hall in Staffordshire this dissuasion involved his trust buying the Hall for one pound, suing the coal board for damages and restoring it themselves. Largely as a result of SAVE's pressure various tax concessions were offered by the government to owners wishing to repair and restore their homes, while at the same time, as the economic climate improved, the property world became aware of the profitability of restoring old mansions or converting them into flats.

Thus the tide has slowly turned. At the time of writing a quarter of the houses in this book have been rescued, and 25 years from now there will be no such thing as a derelict country house. Accidents will continue to happen, like the 1989 fire at Uppark in Sussex, but with a stronger pride in our national heritage the remedy will be swift. Those houses that cannot be restored will be stabilised as ruins, while a few more will, inevitably, be demolished to make way for progress.

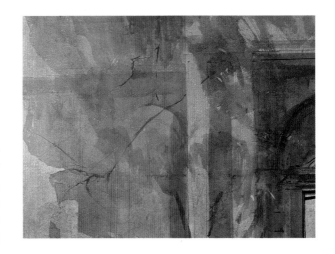

The house hidden in the trees,
Pell Wall Hall – a detail

Vast in conception and extravagant in execution, Witley Court

INTRODUCTION

By Marcus Binney, O.B.E.

Generations of British schoolboys have dreamt of growing. up to be explorers, but as we approach the millennium how many remote fragments of lost civilizations still await discovery? By now every temple in the jungle, every mountain fortress, desert stronghold and island lair has been visited, photographed, measured, and minutely described.

Yet all the time ruins have been accumulating almost unnoticed at home as one fine country house after another has been abandoned to decay. In fiction such empty houses usually have sinister associations, but for those like Alexander Creswell and myself, who make a practice of visiting as many of these silent mansions as we can, the excitement is to find that they are almost always still magical places. Sad they may be, but not frightening.

Osbert Lancaster in a series of cartoons drawn for the V&A exhibition *The Destruction of the Country House*, in 1974 satirized the fate of the great houses of English literature. Mansfield Park had become a girls' school engulfed by flat-roofed classrooms; Disraeli's Bentham crumbled behind Ministry of Defence barbed wire; Peacock's Crotchet Castle was surrounded by gravel pits, while a motorway cut through the avenue at Dickens' Chesneywold.

Yet as I visited more and more of these decaying country houses, particularly those away from the big cities, the excitement was to discover that the setting was only rarely spoilt. Houses like Harleyford, engulfed in caravans, and Stayleybridge with a vast pylon in the back garden, were the exceptions. Again and again houses proved to be in idyllic settings, peaceful, remote, with glorious views, without any ugly development around. True, the park might have been ploughed up, but at least some of the park trees would remain, as well as the shelter belt around the edge. The lawns and terraces were often surprisingly intact, though left to run wild – one new owner cut back the grass in front of the house and found a Morris Minor! Here were Victorian pleasure grounds, or 18th-century wildernesses utterly overgrown, and vast abandoned wall gardens, all of which, with a will could be brought back under control.

In all, SAVE Britain's Heritage has included at least 150 of these houses in a succession of reports – *Tomorrows Ruins, Silent Mansions*

The drawing room fireplace, Ecton Hall – a colour note

and *Endangered Domains* – and north of the border there have been as many again. The most common problem we found was not that the house was beyond repair but that the owner would not sell, at least not on reasonable terms. Indeed, most of these houses, as Sir John Smith, founder of the Landmark Trust, observes are in legal, not financial trouble. There are problems over access – the worst was Scout Hall, near Halifax, where an unsociable neighbour threw nails on the drive when prospective purchasers approached! And there are cases in which the house is offered with insufficient land to protect it – at Crowcombe Court in the Quantocks you could not buy, at one stage, even the yard of lawn around the walls necessary to erect scaffolding.

However, the most outrageous cases were those where local authorities had acquired country houses as amenities, and simply left them to rot. In the first few years the houses would be put to use. Palladian Danson Hill at Bexley Heath, for example, was let for weddings but often even maintenance was neglected and suddenly the house was declared a potential danger and closed. Similar sagas have been played out at Hylands, outside Chelmsford in Essex, which nearly collapsed while councillors argued over whether or not the park could be used as a golf course. While at Highcliffe in Dorset, a perfect example of 1830s picturesque gothic, the Council's contribution to conservation was simply to erect a barbed wire fence around it.

Saving ratepayers' money is one thing. Letting their assets go to rot is another. Yet some councils would prefer to see houses disappear than to allow any private sector organization put them to use. And when, finally, the supposed guardian of the district's heritage agrees to sell, they belatedly decide the place is worth a bomb and suddenly there is no hope of rescuing it without vast new extensions in the grounds.

Quite a number of these houses still belong to their traditional owners, but our experience at SAVE over the past fifteen years is that sooner or later such owners will agree to sell and a solution can be found that is satisfactory to all. Occasionally the owner has moved to a new house nearby and so is particularly sensitive about his new neighbours. Equally he may have had many approaches which have come to nothing and thus grown sceptical.

A great albatross of a house that looks reproachfully at you each morning soon becomes a monster in the imagination. "My house is the ugliest house in the kingdom," one owner raged at me from the porch of his Neo-Georgian villa just across the park from the old mansion. "Every time the Victorian society or some other group of busy bodies writes about it I'm inundated with inquiries from people who want to buy it. Well I'm not selling. I'll keep it weatherproof but no more." Yet this was one of the most handsome Arts and Crafts houses that I have ever seen.

The great baronial pile of Cullen in Banffshire, dating from 1600 but spectacularly aggrandized in the 1840s, presents a similar problem.

Broken windows and shutters ajar, Stocken Hall

Foul graffiti cover the walls, Dunmore House – a detail

The bridge at Edwinsford – a colour note

Following a sale of all the contents in 1975 the house had been closed up and left to its fate. Again and again I was told the owners would never sell. When at last I was able to arrange for Kit Martin and myself to visit the house I unwisely exclaimed as we stepped into the courtyard: "It's magnificent." "One more word from you like that Mr Binney and I'll throw you off the premises," responded the Factor. "I'm sick and tired of historians and art lovers telling me this is a beautiful place. To me it's nothing but a pain." But as we had arrived Kit Martin had noticed a newly-planted hedge along the drive, evidently intended to shut off the old house from the dower house where the family now lived. "That's a good sign. They may be willing to sell," he said. And to our amazement, two hours later we saw the Factor and Lord Seafield pacing out the area of grounds that they might be prepared to sell with the house. Now Cullen is fully restored and occupied. A series of substantial houses – of five bedrooms or more – have been created in the main block, while the kitchen and offices have been adapted as cottages which have been sold to the local schoolteacher and doctor. A whole mixed community has been created.

A few cases, however, are resolved very quickly. Following a strongly-worded press release from SAVE objecting to proposals to demolish Victorian Barrington Court in Essex the house was promptly sold to a local company as its headquarters. But most cases take much longer. The person to object most strongly to an application to demolish Edwardian Llangoed Castle was its architect, 90-year old Sir Clough Williams-Ellis. Although permission was refused the house stood empty for years until eventually, when hope was almost lost, it was sold to Sir Bernard Ashley, husband of the late Laura Ashley, for conversion as a country house hotel.

Similarly, for years every overture made to the owners of Capability Brown's Benham Park, which stood perfectly secluded in a huge car park outside Newbury, was rejected. The pressure to demolish was unrelenting, until suddenly it was sold to a Norwegian computer company which has restored the house as its English headquarters.

At Revesby Abbey in Lincolnshire the saga continues. Here is a delightful very early Victorian house in Elizabethan style, all barley sugar chimneys and fretwork balustrades, which for years defeated all attempts at rescue. Ministers promised to intervene and serve repairs notices, but took four years to take action. Finally, English Heritage was able to send men in directly to repair the roof and halt the decay, and the house was sold to a property company intending to convert it as apartments. But now the local council has refused planning permission. Given the earlier attitude of local councillors this is not altogether surprising but Ministers should have used their powers to decide the matter themselves.

However, there are cases even more wretched than that of Revesby; the houses sold to owners who begin restoration but leave the house in a half-finished state. In 1980 I arrived at Buntingsdale in Shropshire, a splendid example of English baroque, to find a new entrance being crudely hacked through a window and a new off-centre flight of steps destroying the careful symmetry of the elevation. Inside, a new staircase had also been crudely hacked through the ceiling of the large drawing room to the right of the front door. "Don't worry", came the reply from the local planning authority, "when the work is complete you'll be delighted that the house has been given a new lease of life". But the work never was completed. The house was abandoned in a half-finished state, after most of the flats had been sold. The conversion was of unbelievable crudeness – the attics and cellars above and below each unit had simply been sealed off so the owners had no control of what happened around them.

Mavisbank has been an equally protracted saga, but one which shows that determination and persistence produce results. The house stands in a beautiful park just six miles from the centre of Edinburgh, but for years it was surrounded by abandoned caravans and wrecked cars. It was the kind of mess calculated to make councillors cry out: "Get rid of this eyesore. Bulldoze the old pile and let someone build new houses." At one point Mavisbank came within 24 hours of being

An elegant retreat for a man of affairs, Mavisbank House – a detail

Opposite: A fan-vaulted ceiling pulverised by falling masonry, Crawford Priory

The broken front door, Aberpergwm

demolished as a dangerous structure, but court action secured a reprieve and the Lothian Building Preservation Trust has carried out emergency works to stabilize the structure.

In Norfolk, Melton Constable, one of the finest Charles II houses in England and famous as the setting for the film *The Go-Between*, was left to rot year after year by a local farmer who refused to sell. But here was a case where a determined chairman of a local planning committee, waving a repairs notice and making a major fuss in the local press, finally prompted the owner to put the house on the market.

Experience shows that it takes 10 or even 20 years of persistent effort to resolve the plight of many of these houses. How much more could be done if there was a powerfully-motivated unit at English Heritage, fully supported by ministers. The model here should be the highly-successful commission on Venetian villas. In 18 years, between 1952 and 1976, the commission prompted action on more than 400 villas, offering grants, carrying out repairs, and in various particularly extreme cases purchasing houses compulsorily and then reselling them to suitable owners.

Hope for the houses ultimately depends on one simple factor, awareness. Many people, particularly those who have the power to do something about their plight, would rather forget about them. How many junior environment ministers charged with responsibility for listed buildings have come and gone in the last fifteen years while these silent houses have sat decaying? A dozen at least, perhaps twenty. Even as I write the latest has been moved on.

The fact that these houses even in decay make evocative subjects for photography has proved their salvation. Alexander Creswell has added to this record, capturing the atmosphere of the houses in a way the camera rarely can. And when the colour transparencies have long faded, and the photographs survive only in newspaper cuttings and forgotten polemics, his watercolours will live on as a permanent record of one of the romantic quests of our age.

No harm ever came of falling in love with a beautiful building. The magic of these silent houses is that while one walks around them they are entirely one's own. There are no car park attendants, no ticket sellers, no guides discreetly watching as you move from room to room. Here one can explore, free to imagine what was, and what might be. And always there is a frisson of adventure and danger, both from the perilous state of many of the buildings, which must be approached with extreme care, and the possibility that at any moment one's visit might be angrily interrupted.

Just as an ancient site in Turkey where the archaeologists have never excavated and sheep graze across the ruins can be more memorable and evocative than the most carefully-labelled and displayed ancient monument, so these houses, even in a state of decay, retain a compelling fascination.

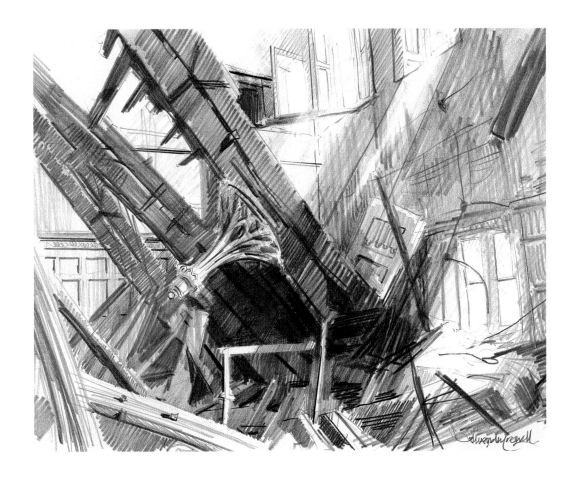

CAVEAT

The locations of the houses in this book have not been revealed. Unless otherwise stated, the houses and their surroundings are private property and they are not open to members of the public.

Those houses that are still unrestored are very dangerous, and no responsibility for injury is accepted by the owners. Permission to visit can only be obtained from the owners or their agents, and in most cases permission would not be forthcoming.

Neither the author nor the publishers can accept any responsibility for any consequences of trespass.

HIGHCLIFFE CASTLE

Dorset   Grade I

Highcliffe was the first and therefore the most striking of all the houses I painted. Now hidden in the middle of a busy resort town on the Dorset coast, it was and is an extraordinary house, not only in its conception and heyday, but also in the gentle atmosphere that pervades it to this day.

As its name would suggest, Highcliffe is indeed perched high above Christchurch Bay and affords distant views to the Isle of Wight. A century ago the Royal family would sail to Highcliffe across the bay from Osborne House, to enjoy its calm sea air and seclusion. Later, Kaiser Wilhelm spent three happy weeks at Highcliffe relaxing after his state visit to Britain, and before the storm-clouds of the Great War loomed on the horizon.

It was as a gentle retreat that Highcliffe was conceived. In the 1820s Lord Charles Stuart de Rothesay was sent as ambassador to Paris after the defeat of Napoleon, and he chanced upon the demolition of a fine house on the Seine. As a keen collector, he purchased many of the architectural features of this house – not just the odd carving or detail, but entire mullion windows and marble doorcases – and from the Abbey of Jumièges he bought a great stained-glass window. Back in England he commissioned the architect, W. Donthorne to design a house around these treasures. The splendid result was a Gothic fantasy that more closely resembled a cathedral than a grand English country residence.

Unfortunately, Lady Stuart was not amused by her husband's choice of house, nor indeed by his architect's design, partly because he omitted to tell her about it until it was almost finished. However, when Lord Stuart died she continued to live there, and eventually left it to her daughter, Lady Waterford.

At the turn of the century Highcliffe was a lively and distinguished household, entertaining the crowned heads of Europe. But by 1950 the house had been sold, and became a children's convalescent home. Three years later it was occupied by the 'Congregation of the Sons of the Immaculate Heart of Mary', who removed the staircase to turn the hall into the chapel that it already resembled.

However, in 1957 there was a fire. Various plans were put forward

Opposite: A carved marble doorcase from France at Highcliffe

to demolish what remained, and for a while it seemed that it would make way for the spread of increasingly-popular seaside bungalows. In the meantime marble fireplaces and fittings were removed and statues stolen, but in 1977 the estate was acquired by the local council. However, the house continued to rot behind its fence, while the remains of the grounds were turned into a cliff-top park.

It seems unlikely that Highcliffe will ever be more than a ruin; it is too small to become an hotel, and too large to be restored as a private house. Under the great *porte-cochère*, reminiscent of Eton chapel, the front door stands ajar, allowing a glimpse of the great hall within; a shaft of sunlight sawing through the vaulted roof picks out a riot of vegetation. On the south side an aged magnolia hangs heavy with bloom, and the smoke from a nearby bonfire ghosts through the mullions. Now calm and endearing in its languor, a Latin inscription on the roof-line reminds one that things could be worse . . .

"Sweet it is, when on the great sea
the winds torment the waters,
to look out from upon the land
on another's terrible struggles".

But the storms do not only cause peril to those at sea; the unprotected gables and towers have loosened over the years and are beginning to fall. Resigned within its protective fence, inhabited only by birds, Highcliffe attracts uncaring glances from the few couples that sit in the park on a summer's afternoon, and gradually crumbles unwitnessed in the teeth of the winter gales.

Under the great *porte-cochère*, Highcliffe

On a summer's afternoon, Highcliffe

At the foot of the staircase, Ashmans Hall

ASHMANS HALL

Suffolk   Grade II

If the gentle seaside resignation found at Highcliffe is representative of the tranquil silence of an empty house, then the atmosphere of Ashmans Hall can only grate on the nerves. From the drive, flanked by the jagged splintered fragments of great beeches flattened in the storm of 1987, the front of the house comes into view. The white brick Regency façade frowns over the remains of a front lawn that is strewn with masonry. While overlooking the garden, a semi-circular bay – like a dustbin with windows – is full of rubble, old fridges and the shattered remains of a glass dome.

The broken front door hangs open revealing a comprehensive picture of decay within – the floors littered with plaster and broken rafters. A strong wind howls through the open rooms, and a nasty feeling creeps up one's back. Somewhere upstairs a broken shutter creaks and slams insistently in the draught; overhead a loose floorboard moves, sending a little salt-shake of dust onto an ever-growing mound.

Gingerly stepping forward into the stair-hall, several startled pigeons escape with a manic slapping of wings, flying up the stairs, clawing the air in a confined space and disappearing through the open roof. In exchange, a ray of sunlight points its thin accusing finger at an obscenity scrawled on the wall – the shiver in the spine becomes too much, and with a degree of urgency one rushes outside into the sunshine, clawing like the pigeons in a rush of claustrophobia. Once back in the car, one feels foolish and courage returns.

Experts describe Ashmans Hall, designed by Robert Rede, c. 1820, in terms of Tuscan colonnades and blind arches; an exceptionally elegant Regency house with a slightly heavy-handed detailing that suggests the work of an amateur architect. The imperial staircase is the most interesting feature – its design probably taken from Worlingham Hall – the cantilevered stone rising in twin arcs to the first floor gallery.

But the powerful incubus within the house seems to render such features irrelevant, just as the falling roof has thrown a column down through the delicate iron balustrade, smashing it onto the floor below. Whether or not one believes in attributing the incomprehensible to the unexplainable, it is difficult not to wonder about the circumstances surrounding the demise of the Robinson family, who once lived here.

Cow parsley at Ashmans Hall

Above: The white brick Regency façade of Ashmans Hall

Opposite: The imperial staircase of cantilevered stone, Ashmans Hall

ASHMAN'S
HALL

MINTO HOUSE

Roxburghshire

Standing at the top of a steep valley into which it is gradually falling, piece by piece, Minto House occupies an impressive position at the centre of an ancient estate in the border country, on the northern slopes of the Cheviot Hills.

There has been a fortified pele tower on this site since the days when the border was fiercely fought over, but in the quieter years in the early part of the last century, the present house was built for the Earl of Minto, Governor-General of India. It was finished in 1814, when the Earl returned from seven years' service in the colony, but unfortunately he died on the journey between London and Scotland, and never saw the new house he had commissioned – only his mortal remains passed through the door.

Minto is of an unusual design; it was built in 1814 to an L-shaped plan, its curved porch standing in the crook of the right-angle. On the garden side the great façades were designed to take best advantage of the views that stretch out to south and west. The whole of the outside of the L measures over 300 feet, and it is a large portion of this that has now cascaded down the valley.

It was the Second World War that marked the end of the house as a home and thereafter up until the 1970s it was used as a school. However, the estate was still owned by Lord Minto, who lived nearby in a new house, and when the school moved out he wanted to demolish the old house, but was refused permission to do so.

Since then it has simply remained empty, and has gradually fallen to bits. Now there is no roof left and the drive in front of the porch is being used to store hay. The garden is completely overgrown, much of the park has been given over as a golf course for Minto village, and many of the trees in the grounds, some of which were over 250 years old and included among their number a few of the tallest larches in the country, have now been felled.

As the old house crumbles away, so do any hopes that it will ever be restored; the family will not sell it, and so the old stones continue to roll down into the stream. Instead of being the nucleus of its estate, it is gently reverting to nature – becoming merely an untidy back-drop to the golf course.

Above: A curved porch standing in the crook of a right-angle, Minto House

Opposite: A large part of the façade cascaded into the valley, Minto House

The drive lined with flowering fireweed, High Head Castle

HIGH HEAD CASTLE

Cumbria   Grade II*

The over-riding impression of High Head Castle in the summer is that of the colour red; the drive is lined with flowering fireweed, the bright willowherb a dusty red that strengthens as the trees recede. As the façade comes into view the fireweed reaches a crescendo against a backdrop of deep sienna. This red sandstone, unique to the area, is itself accentuated by a contrasting flash of lush green ivy.

In 1744 Henry Richmond Brougham returned from the Grand Tour of Europe to inherit a decaying Tudor stone farmhouse perched on a crag in the Cumbrian hills. Enlisting the assistance of his uncle, an amateur architect, Brougham set about designing himself something more suitable, and demolished most of the old house. His designs produced a magnificent Georgian house in the Gibbs style, that even now is considered to be the finest house of the period in Cumbria. The building of the new High Head was finished in 1749, but Brougham never saw it – he died the same year, unmarried and childless.

In 1921 the house was shown in its fine original state to the readers of *Country Life*, as the home of Major John Hills MP. But in 1956 it was gutted by fire. All of the 18th-century interiors were destroyed, and over the ensuing 30 years of solitude everything moveable was pillaged.

Climbing the twin steps to the front door one can now walk unhindered through the house. By leaning on the window ledge in what was once the dining room one can appreciate the extent of the spectacular view to the south; Brougham built his house on the brink of a chasm that falls down a sheer 100 feet to a chuckling trout stream below.

The silhouette of High Head towers over the scene – a pink Acropolis taken from a burning Turner sunset, or a Dionysian temple from a Claude Lorraine landscape. In the bed of the stream lie fragments of balustrade, brought crashing down from their precarious perch on the roofless parapet above.

Half of the house is now covered with a cascade of ivy, the rapacious fingers of which insinuate themselves between the well-laid stones. Winter ice expands the cracks, ensuring that the gales will eventually succeed in toppling yet more masonry. Soon the pieces of balustrade in the gorge will be joined by sections of cornice and parts of the upper walls, as High Head Castle disintegrates.

Among the tall weeds on the steps, High Head Castle

COPPED HALL

Essex Grade II

The fire that destroyed Copped Hall in 1917 was thought to have been started by a hairclip, which had been hastily used to replace an electrical fuse. The first smoke was noticed by the household on the morning of Sunday the 5th of May as the family prepared to go to church, and was largely ignored, the servants removing some articles of value before the blaze spread unchecked. Firemen with horse-drawn engines and an inadequate water supply struggled in vain, and the interior was soon destroyed; the heat had been so intense that for days later the cellars echoed with the popping of exploding wine bottles.

To anyone who has travelled along the London orbital motorway, the shell of Copped Hall is a familiar landmark, by sight if not by name. It was built in the mid-18th century at the edge of Epping Forest, an ornament in the landscape which its architect John Sanderson would have been proud of. But it is now a ruin that stares vacantly onto the teeming motorway that has severed it from its parkland and the forest.

The Wythes family who were driven out by the fire were not the first household to be dissolved, nor was Sanderson's Hall the first building to be destroyed at Copped. The name 'Coppedehalle' originates from 1258, when a house stood on a cop, or solitary hill. In 1350 Copped passed to the Abbots of Waltham, and later it was offered to King Henry VIII as an unsuccessful bribe to save their abbey from dissolution.

The young Edward VI later gave the estate to his half-sister, Mary Tudor; Mary was heir to the throne, but she was Catholic and Edward's parliament was Protestant, so her occupation of Copped Hall was as a prisoner. When she succeeded to the throne in 1553, she granted the lease of Copped to the Duchy of Lancaster, and in 1558 both the throne and Copped Hall passed to Queen Elizabeth. But the estate had been exploited by its tenants, and the buildings were ruinous. Queen Elizabeth gave the estate to her friend and counsellor Thomas Heneage, who rebuilt the Hall. It is said that, when Heneage married the Countess of Southampton, the first performance of Shakespeare's *A Midsummer Night's Dream* was given in the Long Gallery at Copped.

By the mid-18th century the fine Tudor mansion was once again neglected and derelict. This time a new house was built by Edward Conyers MP, to the designs of John Sanderson, and within three gener-

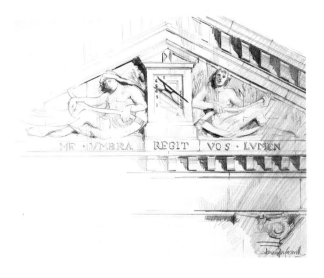

Above: *'Me umbra regit. . .'*, a sundial on the pediment, Copped Hall

Opposite: The pavilion in the light of a full moon, Copped Hall

ations the estate was sold to George Wythes. As a wealthy tycoon of the early Victorian 'railway madness' he immediately started a programme of extension and refurbishment; a staff wing and a conservatory were added, and fine gardens were laid out – a jigsaw of terraces, parterres and borders, embellished with Italianate statues, obelisks and balustrades. The two pavilions flanking the main terrace are delightfully eclectic, incorporating the diluted Palladianism of the house, with fantastic touches of Jacobean and bacchanalian ornamentation.

Wythes' expenses on Copped Hall amounted to £17,000, a considerable sum at a time when a house in London cost around £200. Today the gardens are now an unrecognizable echo of their former extravagance. A large sundial on the pediment of the house proclaims: *'me umbra regit vos lumen'* – 'I am ruled by shadow, you by light' – a sad testament to the glory of Wythes' garden, now chokingly overgrown.

Country Life magazine once advised its readers that 'every room of the principal storey of Copped Hall demands attention', but now it is hard to differentiate between the principal floor and the basement. Not a ceiling remains, nor a fragment of the decoration. Also lost were fine chairs upholstered in silk from the Borghese Palace, paintings by Hobbema and Reynolds, and antique Chinese wall–hangings.

To be at Copped Hall must really have been '. . . to learn in most agreeable fashion the lessons of the architectural and decorative arts in England from the 16th to the 20th centuries' – again, *Country Life*. Yet now, sadly it is impossible to penetrate the deep mass of brambles inside.

A familiar landmark, the shell of Copped Hall

A pavilion at Copped Hall

Proud protruding towers and gables, Buchanan Castle

BUCHANAN CASTLE

Stirlingshire   Category B

On a slight hill on the eastern shores of Loch Lomond stands the shell of a great Scottish seat, its towers and gables protruding proudly above the trees of its domain. A flock of white doves circles in alarm as an intruder paces about outside its protective fence, which safeguards it from the new inhabitants of the park. Once set in splendid seclusion, yet enjoying a tremendous view to the south and west, the parkland has now been given over to a golf course, and the area immediately surrounding the house has been rudely invaded by a rash of modern bungalows.

At the back of Buchanan Castle

A semi-circular Romeo balcony over the entrance is flanked by elegant statues of storks taken from the Montrose crest, their former dignity now streaked with white from the doves roosting above. Buchanan Castle had been the principal seat of the dukes of Montrose from the mid-17th century onwards. The second Duke married Lady Lucy Manners, the daughter of the Duke of Rutland, and when he first brought her to Buchanan to his surprise the new bride burst into tears, saying that the landscape was so bare and cold compared to her native Belvoir. The Duke immediately sent for 'Capability' Brown, and commissioned him to lay out a park that was second to none. These grounds existed until 1939, at which point all the trees were felled.

In 1852 the old house was destroyed in a fire, and the fourth Duke built the present house in true Scottish Baronial style. At the ceremony of the laying of the foundation stone, coins and journals were buried underneath and a great party was held for the builders; the Duke provided quantities of ale saying that 'no stone however well laid would take bond without moisture'. In the 1920s, thirteen bathrooms were added, and the family wintered there every year until 1934.

Subsequently the castle was rented by Cunard for the entertainment of American clients, but it was requisitioned in the War for use as a hospital with no less than a thousand beds. In the 1950s Buchanan was considered in the search for a suitable building in which to house the Burrell Collection, but since it was too far from Glasgow the plan failed. The castle was subsequently unroofed to exempt it from rates and when the housing estate was built the future was secured – never again would Buchanan be inhabited, and so it has been left to gradually fall down.

CARADOC COURT

Herefordshire   Grade II*

The earliest resident of the estate of Cradock, or Caradock, was reputed to have been a British chieftain, Knight of King Arthur's Table and folklore hero called *Vraich-Vras* (tr. 'Strong Arm'). From 1594 the estate belonged to the now-extinct Viscounts Scudamore, a century later to the Digby family and in 1929 was acquired in its present form by Lt. Col. George Heywood.

Surprisingly, Caradoc appears to be essentially two houses; to the north side there is the black-and-white timber-framed house of the 16th century, and to the south, a stone house of 1620. The Victorian urge to decorate and embellish has left the building remarkably handsome with its neo-Jacobean façade and the older part of the house unaltered.

A blustery day in February was a perfect time to visit the hollow shell. The gates swung open easily and under a darkening sky the reddish stonework came into view, glistening after a heavy shower. Looking across the formal garden, now just grass, the façade was suddenly lit up by a theatrical flood of afternoon sunlight, as dramatic in contrast as in its clarity. Now the colour of the stone sang, and the sun fragmented off broken windows. Against the blue, the collapsed gables and empty mullions stood in sharp relief.

From the other side, the house balanced precariously above a steep escarpment, its vertiginous position amplifying the delight of the distant views it affords; the valley of the River Wye extending far below and the Welsh hills looming in the distance. Across the front of this Elizabethan part of the house runs a long terrace bounded by a yew hedge – a narrow parapet before the cliff. Tidy lawns and trim hedges attest to the care taken to preserve Caradoc. It is lying in state, waiting for the next life – full of hope even in dereliction.

In spite of this outward charm, the shambles of the interior was a discordant sight. Fire had destroyed everything, only the Morning Room showed panelling that had escaped, buried deep beneath rubble and beams. In the former grand hall, a stone fireplace had been chipped by falling masonry, and the arcade of the gallery supported only an iron pipe. But nothing remained of the room in the attic that once boasted a painted 17th-century ceiling. Halfway up one wall, balancing on a beam, was an old bath full of weeds.

Above: The Victorian neo-Jacobean façade, Caradoc

Opposite: Collapsed gables and empty mullions against the sky, Caradoc

The timber-framed 16th-century house, Caradoc

The garden gates swung open, Caradoc

The owner's caravan in front of Kirklinton

KIRKLINTON HALL

Cumbria   Grade II

A few miles from the Scottish border stands Kirklinton Hall, well hidden in its farmland. Invisible from the road, the presence of the house is suggested only by a tumbledown iron gate in a quiet lane. Beyond it a muddy track curves away through the trees. An unlikely entrance it seemed, but picking a way carefully between the puddles with geese hissing aggressively at one's ankles, the house suddenly comes into view. Originally it was a Georgian block that was extended in 1875, with the addition of a large wing and the embellishment of the whole with mock-Jacobean gables and finials. It was dryly described by Pevsner as 'all rather bleak'.

Bleak it certainly is; the roof has fallen in taking the floors with it, and the garden is littered with the carcasses of old cars and washing machines. A limp clothes-line is festooned with tatty underwear, and the whole place looks like a gypsy camp. The reason for all this became clear as the owner appeared in the doorway of his caravan looking very cross, and evidently not keen to receive uninvited visitors.

After the War Kirklinton was a country club, but was subsequently sold to an individual who wanted to turn the house into flats. No work started, and in 1982 the local council received an application for permission to demolish the Hall. As a Grade II listed building, this permission was refused.

In many cases, when an owner wants to demolish a house without consent, the easiest thing to do is simply to let nature gradually demolish it for you and hope that nobody sees. This was evidently the policy at Kirklinton; the owner was living right outside the front door in his caravan, and therefore was in a good position to prevent anyone coming too close or seeing too much.

The gate at the entrance looked no different to that of a neglected copse, and if anyone did stray onto the land the geese kept an alert vigil. Any idea of painting the Hall was completely out of the question.

A little while later, braving the geese a second time, I managed to rough a brief sketch of the façade and its accoutrements. But suddenly the figure appeared again at his door with a shotgun in his hand, and emptied it in my general direction as I hurried off into the lane, cursing the geese for their legendary efficiency as guardians.

The guardians of Kirklinton

A gaunt silhouette from across the river, Guy's Cliffe

GUY'S CLIFFE

Warwickshire   Grade II

In a sandstone cliff flanking a graceful bend in the river Avon at Warwick, there once lived a hermit called Guy. He was a large man, his stature magnified by legend, who fell in love with the fair Felice, daughter of the Saxon Earl of Warwick. But Guy's lowly birth made him unacceptable to Felice and her father unless, that is, he could prove his worth. After fighting in Normandy and on the Crusades, and by slaughtering with his bare hands a fearsome dun cow that was terrifying the neighbourhood, he successfully wooed her and they were married – the Earl and Countess of Warwick. With more to do, he returned to fight on further Crusades, winning countless battles against the infidels.

When he returned to England, weak and disillusioned, Guy of Warwick chose to wean himself from the 'deceitful pleasures of this world', and retired to the solitary calm of his cave in the cliff to pass the remainder of his days. He ventured out only to take food from Felice, who took pity on this poor hermit whom she never recognized. Before he died he sent her their wedding ring, telling her that she would find him in front of the altar in the chapel on top of the cliff – dead. On finding him, the devoted Countess threw herself from the clifftop above Guy's cave.

The present house at Guy's Cliffe was built in 1751, growing out of and above the great cliffs. In 1822 it was considerably extended by Mr Bertie Greatheed, who added a new entrance front and extended the rooms inside, and through his daughter the estate passed to the Percys, the dukes of Northumberland.

In the 1920s Guy's Cliffe was admired by all who visited its last noble owner, Lord Algernon Percy. When he died in 1933, the family gathered from Alnwick for the funeral. The last Duke, as a young man, quietly took the opportunity to go for a day's hunting nearby, thereby flouting the proprieties of mourning. The next day before his uncle's funeral, in the hall at Guy's as he unpacked his hat, his spurs clattered onto the marble floor. His father's disapproving frown was reprimand enough and at the graveside the latter leant over and, with a glint in his eye, asked his uncompliant son whether he had seen any good woodcock the day before.

The funeral was the last time that Guy's Cliffe was occupied as a

The back door and courtyard, Guy's Cliffe

home. During the Second World War it became a school for evacuees, and was later bought by speculators who unsuccessfully tried to develop its impressive site. The house was unroofed and in 1952 the contents auctioned; by 1974 the structure of the building was in a precarious state; some parts had collapsed, although the chapel remained complete. At this time the property was owned by the Provincial Senior Grand Warden of the local Freemasons, and he offered it to the Coventry Lodges, who needed a suitable meeting place. The rent was two bottles of beer annually. Guy's Cliffe offered the ideal surroundings to the Masons, and they transformed its 15th-century chapel of St Mary Magdalene into their temple. Its interior is now adorned with the peculiar paraphernalia of Masonic ritual. In the early 1980s the owner died, and the Masons bought the property, and now gradually attempt to restore what parts of the house they can with the funds available.

Inside the empty frame of Guy's Cliffe, high up where the third floor once was, an iron mantelpiece spins slowly in the breeze, suspended only by the bell-cord. While in the shambles of the drawing room the remains of an ornate plaster alcove stands on its own, the wall having collapsed behind it. The iron balustrade of the stairs bulges like the rib-cage of a dead beast – its guts the rotten timbers fallen from above. The house stands as a gaunt silhouette from across the river, its crumbling walls and sinister caves giving the masons the seclusion that they require.

The principal door, Guy's Cliffe – a colour note

The stairs at Guy's Cliffe

Above the mud of rotten wood, foul graffiti cover the walls of Dunmore

DUNMORE HOUSE

Stirlingshire   Category B

Dunmore House was built by William Wilkins in 1829, his last Tudor-Gothic country house. Designed around a central courtyard, the principal rooms and the service quarters are all linked by a continuous corridor, like a cloister. The estate was run, and the house occupied, by the earls of Dunmore; the seventh Earl being a keen and forward-thinking agriculturalist who invented the steam-plough. A contemporary photograph shows him at Dunmore with his invention – a vast contraption that looks more like the Flying Scotsman than a simple farm plough.

Later shunned by the family, the house became a girls' school that existed until the last war. It has since remained empty and is now owned by a local farmer whose interest stretches only to the removal and re-use of the stone from the service wing. All the fine elements of the interior have been removed and the ceilings have begun to fall in. Little plaster-work remains, the fireplaces have gone and the doorcases are broken. Outside, the terraces are overgrown with sapling birch trees, and ivy covers the *porte-cochère*.

These crumbling houses are constantly enshrouded in a profound smell of damp and rot, and at Dunmore on a crisp autumn day this heady smell hung in the air, readily identifiable from a distance. But inside the rotten hulk of panelled rooms the more familiar redolence of urine wrinkles the nose; it seems that as a dog marks its presence, so some primitive bestial instinct causes the simple-minded to defecate and urinate when they find themselves where they shouldn't be. Above the mud of rotten wood and plaster, foul graffiti cover the walls, and in corners groups of old cider bottles huddle where they were thrown by the inebriated.

Through the woods, half-a-mile away, the now-famous 'Pineapple' stands in its restored splendour. Once this extraordinary fruit-shaped folly also stood derelict, attracting the attentions of vandals from nearby Grangemouth. However, thankfully it was acquired by the National Trust for Scotland and is now maintained by the Landmark Trust. The 'Pineapple' can be rented for holiday accommodation, but few who stay there are aware of the presence of the main house as it gradually decomposes nearby.

Ivy covering the *porte-cochère*, Dunmore

A giant portico and curved wing leading to the orangery, Witley Court

WITLEY COURT

Worcestershire   Grade I

Witley Court today is by far the most impressive country house ruin in existence in Britain. Nearly a century ago it stood comparison with Blenheim Palace or Castle Howard, and in its development, heyday and subsequent demise, Witley Court is archetypal of the extremes of fortune of great families during the last hundred years.

Since the 13th century the estate of Witley has been enlarged and altered, its ownership passing from descendants of the Normans to the industrialists of the post-Civil War era; the Foleys, for example, held the property for 180 years until their entrepreneurial fortunes were squandered by the gambling of 'Lord Balloon', the obese third Lord Foley, and the house at Witley had to be sold to meet crippling debts.

With a vast wealth gleaned from mining and ironworking activities at the height of the Industrial Revolution, it was the Viscounts Dudley who acquired Witley in 1837, for today's equivalent sum of 40 million pounds. Lord William Ward, later the first Earl of Dudley, was only twenty-one when he bought Witley, but it was not until seven years later that he started to transform the house into the Palladian palace that it was to become.

Vast in conception and extravagant in execution, the existing Witley was augmented by a wing on either side of the front entrance, creating a deep courtyard and, in the garden, a giant portico and a curved wing leading to the orangery. The ground-plan is extensive, the scale colossal and the features grand, but nowhere is the style anything but restrained; the stone facing of the house and chapel is simple but not bold, very unlike the contemporary High Victorian trends, refreshing as a consequence and a credit to the architect, Samuel Dawkes.

To the south of the Court, extensive, formal Italianate gardens were laid out, enclosed by a stone balustrade with gazebos at its corners. The most flamboyant features of the garden are two giant fountains; to the south the Poseidon Fountain, some 20 tons of sculpted stone depicting Perseus saving Andromeda from Poseidon's monster, and featuring a jet of water over 100 feet high; to the east the Triton Fountain, by way of contrast, is an altogether more modest affair.

In its heyday Witley Court entertained a highly-fashionable society – the second Earl was a great friend of the Prince of Wales, later King

The steps to the main door, Witley Court

Edward VII, who enjoyed the sporting opportunities of the estate and the hospitality of the house. Consequently it became a byword for gracious living, exemplary in late Victorian and Edwardian high society. But even the massive wealth of the Dudley's waned towards the end of the 1890s, and during the depression after the First World War the second Earl went into debt. Soon after, the final blow was struck by fate when the Countess died tragically in a drowning accident in 1921. The Earl sold the entire estate – the Court itself and nine thousand acres of land. The grandeur that was Witley had started on its decline.

A carpet magnate from Kidderminster, Sir Herbert Smith, bought the Court, and trimmed its extravagance in accordance with the economic climate; thus electricity was introduced and the heating system redesigned – formerly some 30 tons of coal had been needed to heat the house for just one day! But then on a September evening in 1937 a fire broke out in one of the kitchens and spread unchecked, engulfing the east wing and part of the central block. The opulent interiors of the ballroom and royal apartments were lost in their entirety to the blaze which the skeleton staff were unable to contain.

The greater part of the main house, together with the outbuildings and chapel, were spared by the blaze, but in the shadow of the impending war Smith sold the estate at auction for a mere £21,000, the land being sold separately and the Court and its grounds acquired by demolition contractors. Over the next 40 years the Court was stripped, and in 1972 it was taken into the care of the Department of the Environment.

The great fountains – once the bold *pièce-de-resistance* of the Earls of Dudley and the embodiment of their era – now stand as silent monuments to that time, and perhaps as a respectful reminder of the Countess of Dudley, whose drowning sadly heralded the end of the 'Palace of Witley'.

The Court is now open to the public, and it is well worth the journey to marvel at the skeleton of this magnificent house, set in the grassy remains of the Italian gardens. The fountains are now dry, and the orangery glass-less. Only the chapel is complete and restored to its former glory – the finest Baroque church in the country. It is by reference to this grand interior that one can perhaps visualise how Witley Court might once have been.

The Poseidon Fountain, 20 tons of sculpted stone, Witley Court

The steps from the courtyard, Witley Court

ABERGLASNEY

Carmarthenshire

Deep within the core of Aberglasney lie the remains of a medieval house, which was demolished as long ago as 1600 when a new mansion was built for Bishop Anthony Rudd. Today its primitive cloisters survive in the garden. The present house is architecturally and historically puzzling, but one thing is certain – it is not a handsome building. The original bishop's mansion was extended and modernised in the early 18th century by the family of John Dyer, the poet. The results of their expenditure were inspiration enough to their famous son; as he sat on a nearby hill he wrote:

> *"See below the pleasant dome*
> *The poet's pride, the poet's home,*
> *Which the sunbeams shine upon*
> *To the even from the dawn.*
> *See the woods where echo talks,*
> *Her gardens trim, her terrace walks,*
> *Her wildernesses, fragrant brakes,*
> *Her gloomy bowers and shining lakes.*
> *Keep ye Gods this humble seat*
> *For ever pleasant, private, neat."*

Of course it is all very different nowadays. There is no sign of the pleasant dome and the splendid gardens have almost disappeared, the terrace walks on top of Rudd's vaulted cloisters are only just discernible, and the once shining lakes are just swampy meadows by the banks of the river Towi.

The original Dyer house was based around a courtyard, but later extensions added a jumble of extra rooms and the form was lost. A pompous portico was added in the last century, but it now leans against the front of the house like a drunk. Inside the entrance is a fine two-storeyed hall, but that is now full of junk. In one of the principal rooms a small stream springs in the fireplace and flows across the floor and out under an exterior wall towards what is left of the gardens. In its damp and gloomy valley, Aberglasney continues to gradually disintegrate like wet newspaper.

Opposite: Aberglasney disintegrates in its damp gloomy valley

'Keep ye Gods this humble seat, For ever pleasant, private, neat', Aberglasney

A fine two-storeyed hall full of junk, Aberglasney

The river was a swollen torrent under the old bridge, Edwinsford

EDWINSFORD HOUSE

Carmarthenshire   Grade II

Over the hills some miles from Aberglasney, Edwinsford House nestles in the valley on the banks of the Cothi. It was an important gentry house, built in the 17th century and consisting of two separate houses built corner to corner. Architecturally it is of great interest, illustrating two very different forms of 17th-century planning; in one part the house is built around the central staircase, and in the other, the chimney forms the central axis of the building, with all the fireplaces backing onto it. The house was considerably enlarged in the 19th century, and the entrance façade was adorned with a Victorian porch.

Despite a fierce notice warning of imminent danger to all who venture inside, Edwinsford now looks simply sad and forlorn. The interior was obviously once magnificent; the elaborate coffered plaster-work of Carolean ceilings miraculously survive in the one half of the building, while the roof of the other has now fallen in, crushing all beneath it, and the dining-room, of lovely proportions, has been used to store hay – it is strange to see a barn with an ornate 17th-century plaster ceiling! During the War, Polish refugees grew mushrooms under the floorboards in the drawing-room, and now brambles have crept in through the windows to prize up whatever is left of the floor.

Saplings grow out of the roof, and virginia creeper has almost obliterated the front façade, but the house still has beautiful views up the valley. The former extensive and well-kept gardens that once hosted rare South American plants, are now just a tangled mass of grass and weeds. A graceful stone bridge arcs over the babbling river as it rushes down a series of little rapids past Edwinsford through the rolling Welsh hills, which rise majestically on either side of the house.

A year later I passed Edwinsford during a full gale. The river was a raging swollen torrent that threatened to wash away the old bridge and the trees groaned and strained to stay upright on its brimming banks. An old cupboard door cartwheeled across the grass in the teeth of the wind, ending its journey in a shrub yards away down the garden. A chimney had already fallen and crashed through the surviving ceilings, landing in the hay where I had once sat. From the roof, slates flew like lethal missiles that embedded themselves in a nearby cow-field. It was time to bid farewell to Edwinsford.

An important gentry-house, Edwinsford

The ornamental canal and Georgian façade, Stocken Hall

STOCKEN HALL

Leicestershire   Grade II*

Stocken Hall looks inhabited, but like an old photograph it is suspended in time, slightly decrepit. In the garden, the grass is mown, the shrubs pruned and the ornamental canal still full of water, with lilies thriving in the sun. The oldest part of the house is Georgian, dating from the early 17th century, but it was re-worked by George Portwood of Stamford in the 18th century. On its principal façade the windows are all closed, some with shutters ajar and some broken. It feels as though whoever lives there is too tired to open the house to the warm spring sunshine, resigned instead to lurk in the shadows within.

But the front door is padlocked and boarded up – the house is empty, and has been for many years. In the musty old drawing room, a long finger of sunlight moves imperceptibly across the floor, like the hands of a clock, as the sun gently travels westward and finally roosts in the branches of an ancient beech tree. A pile of leaves that have blown in through a broken pane make a little compost heap in a damp corner.

Looking out of the windows and over the rolling fields one can see immediately why the house is empty; a high wire fence surrounds the garden, and some way away a modern housing development provides accommodation for prison officers, for Stocken's former estate is now a prison farm. The Hall is in the centre of the complex and is cut off from the rest of the world. Beyond the fence, the inmates go about their quotidian tasks and one sits under a tree sketching the Hall in a tireless and meticulous style, as another day drifts slowly by.

Stocken was requisitioned by the RAF in 1940, and after the War the Home Office took it over. They shut up the house and used the farm to provide work for the inmates from nearby Ashwell prison. New buildings went up in the grounds as the prison expanded, and in 1980 the Home Office decided to demolish Stocken. After long negotiations they were persuaded to offer it for sale instead; but who would buy a dilapidated house in the middle of a prison? With limited access and little adjoining land, it became certain that Stocken would never be a private house again – indeed, it is to be a nursing home.

So the period of emptiness is over. The shutters will be thrown open, the sunlight will pour in and the leaves will be swept out. Stocken will leap into the present, its 45-year sentence of solitude expired.

A long finger of sunlight in the drawing room, Stocken Hall

OULTON HALL

Yorkshire Grade II

There are few pleasant surprises in the grey industrial sprawl around the city of Leeds. To the west of the city, the ruins of Kirkstall Abbey stand as a monument to its importance before the reign of Henry VIII and in the rolling landscape to the east Oulton Park serves to remind one of the industrial boom that put Leeds on the map during the early years of the 19th century. If the park surprises by its existence in this 'Lowry-esque' urban environment, then it is thanks to its creator, Humphrey Repton.

A modest house on the hill, above what in 1820 was Oulton village, was bought by a wealthy Leeds merchant, John Blayds, and a fine new mansion was built for him by the architect Robert Smirke. The landscape around it was created by Repton, and for its design he made one of his legendary 'red books'. With the Park laid and planted, and a new church built at the bottom of the hill, the ensemble was complete – a happy, and often only too rare, combination of a wealthy client engaging the best designers of the day.

After a fire some 25 years later, Smirke's brother, Sydney, rebuilt the interior of the house, and the whole estate survived until the Second World War. At Kirkstall, Leeds City Council bought and stabilized the old ruined abbey, now proudly displayed on their tourist posters, but at Oulton, neglect by the County Council has been largely responsible for the loss of a fine estate. They used it as a mental hospital until 1974, and five years later tried to demolish it, rather than spend £4000 on roof repairs. The church went to the parish, and the park was turned into a golf course, but the house was left to rot to the torturous echoes of a dripping roof.

Although all the stonework is as crisp as the day it was cut, its original honey colour has inevitably been blackened with soot from the factory chimneys. The once-fine interiors have been smashed and pillaged and the trappings of the mental hospital still abound; crude enamel signs survive, screwed to the plasterwork, directing the unfortunates to their wards – 'isolation' or 'theatre'. Bars on the windows, sometimes bent, and a broken handrail at the top of the stairs, seem to cry out in desperation. These, and a rusty iron bed are all that remain of the cuckoo's nest.

Above: Crisp stonework on the portico of Oulton Hall

Opposite: Looking into the stair hall at Oulton

REVESBY ABBEY

Lincolnshire   Grade I

The magnificent 'Jacob-ethan' mansion built for J. Banks Stanhope in 1844 was called Revesby Abbey in reverence to the 12th-century Cistercian monastery, on the site of which it stands. Designed by the prolific Scottish architect and pioneer of the Jacobean revival, William Burn, Revesby Abbey survives in its entirety due to its strength of construction.

The estate was once owned by the botanist Sir Joseph Banks, who gave his name to many species of plant, notably the Banksii rose, and after voyaging with Captain Cook earned the soubriquet, 'Father of Australia'. The present house was built by the family after his death, and remains at the centre of the estate. After the Second World War, Revesby was used as flats for American servicemen from a nearby airbase, but most recently it has remained empty.

Revesby Abbey is definitely not open to the public, and stands in the middle of its deer park. Peering through the great iron gates, the gables and chimneys can be made out among the trees, just like those of a flourishing estate. It is this seclusion that has ensured a merciful survival, far from the hands of vandals. On closer inspection the exuberant exterior comes into view – embellished with rich strap work on the porch and ornamental carving on the gables; such crisp stonework bodes well for the future condition of a house that has been unoccupied for over 30 years.

Amazingly the roof is intact and hardly a pane of glass is broken. Within the principal rooms a dusty silence has settled over this fragile time-capsule – the once-extravagant German Baroque and Louis XV interiors now only play host to a mouse, whose scurrying progress around the panelling is amplified by the cavernous emptiness; while overhead, the Viennese plasterwork crumbles like stale cake, and on the windowsill lies a clutch of desiccated corpses – roosting pigeons that were unable to escape.

Suddenly a distant flapping upstairs stirs uneasy feelings . . . a door stands open to the hall, inviting, admonishing and then forbidding . . . something flutters on the darkened stairs beyond . . . it's time to leave. Once again the silence falls, almost visible in the shafts of sunlight that percolate through the murky windows.

Rich strap work on the porch, Revesby

Above: A detail of carving in the library, Revesby

Opposite: A dusty silence in the principal rooms, Revesby

A shroud of ivy obliterating the façade of Poltalloch

POLTALLOCH HOUSE

Argyll   De-listed

New Poltalloch from the fields

Almost as far to the west as one can go on mainland Argyll lies the little fishing village of Crinan. Made famous by Telford's great canal that cuts through from Loch Fyne to the open sea, Crinan now boasts an hotel with superb views over to the islands Scarba and Jura. On a wet and windy October day the coast was enshrouded in mist and thin driving rain, and one could barely see the grey silhouette of Duntrune Castle across the loch.

The legend of the siege of Duntrune set the scene for the hunt for Poltalloch House: in 1615 the castle belonged to the Campbell clan and had been captured by the hostile MacDonalds. While the latter's chief was away in Islay, the Campbells stormed the castle and killed all within, save only the piper – it being considered unlucky to kill a piper. When the chief of the MacDonalds returned, sailing up the sound of Jura, the gallant piper played a hasty lament on the battlements to warn his master. The warning was heeded and the MacDonalds withdrew. The Campbells, realizing what had happened, cut off the piper's fingers so that he should never play again. But he bled to death and his body was disposed of under the flagstones in the castle. During the last century, while the castle was being modernized, a skeleton was found under the floor – it had no fingers!

A long time before the siege, the first Celtic warriors from the kingdom of Dalraida settled in the meadows of the banks of the River Add, and the surrounding hills are now scattered with their strange standing-stones and cairns, considered to be the most impressive in Britain. On such an ancient stage the tales of Poltalloch, Old and New, are short indeed.

It was suitable that on another wet and dismal day the search for the ruins of the two Poltallochs was undertaken. The first expedition – for so it seemed – led through an endless dripping forest of conifers. The weather closed in further, threatening and wild. The track tightened, irrevocably falling towards a distant loch. Suddenly a glade opened up, revealing a misty view westwards. In the foreground nestled the black stones of Old Poltalloch.

It was here that the Malcolms of Duntrune settled in the 1790s. Today their house is no more than a few walls in the rain, as nature and the Forestry Commission reclaim the hillside. By the middle of the last century the Malcolms had moved back towards Crinan and, on the grassy meadows of the Add, had built a large and strangely-English, Jacobean mansion. Its warm stone, crisply carved, and its gables and strap work are all reminiscent of Revesby Abbey – for both were designed by William Burn.

Now the rich stone is splashed with lichen and moss, a patina of algal growth that thrives in the warm winds of the Gulf Stream. On the south side a shroud of ivy has all but obliterated the façade, smothering the stonework, and loosening the mortar. Pieces of gable and parapet already lie in the cellars, and in the orangery fragments of hand-glazed tiles can be found underfoot. Cattle wander freely on the terraces, the ornate stone ballustrade that once kept them out has now been better employed to embellish the garden at Duntrune. The staff accomodation on a sunken level at the back of the house, formerly the size of a small village, is now an impenetrable forest of birch and thorn.

In the summer months the shell of Poltalloch seems like an amusing folly amongst stands of beech. Great mature rhododendrons flower profusely in spring and the park looks well-groomed as it descends to the sea. But in the winter, as storms lash the coast and the incessant rain turns the meadow to marsh, Poltalloch's shell seems strangely out of place – its delicate detailing and Victorian exuberance incompatible with the history of the Western Highlands; so now New Poltalloch too becomes just stones in the rain, a mere 150 years after it was built.

The black stones of Old Poltalloch

The rich stone splashed with lichen, Poltalloch

The drawing room fireplace rises above a heap of plaster, Ecton

ECTON HALL

Northamptonshire   Grade II

The idea of an empty crumbling house is often synonymous with that of the haunted house so overplayed in the early days of cinema. Indeed, many houses, empty or otherwise, are thought to be overrun with the restless spirits of previous incumbents. Therefore, it will no doubt be bad news to any future inhabitants of Ecton Hall to reveal the aged curse that brought about the eventual demise of the house, earlier this century.

Ecton stands in the pastoral Northamptonshire countryside, an early 18th-century mansion reworked in a Gothic style in 1756, but its origins firmly rooted in the 16th century. At some time in its history the curse is reputed to have threatened that all who lived in Ecton should remain childless. However, the estate passed through various branches of the Sotheby family, until the death of Lady Sotheby in 1952. Surely enough, she died childless, and the estate was taken into the hands of trustees. Unfortunately, whilst retaining the outbuildings and sur-rounding land, the trust allowed the house itself to gradually fall into a state of disrepair.

The pastoral Northamptonshire countryside around Ecton Hall

Soon after the death of Lady Sotheby, builders were called in to demolish a large kitchen extension and took the opportunity to spirit away the lead from the roof. This of course introduced the first footholds for decay. The rich ochre stone of the garden front is engulfed in Virginia creeper, and sparkles of broken glass litter the terrace. Inside the house, the drawing-room fireplace rises above a heap of plaster that the roof has brought down, and an old picture frame is propped against one wall, its canvas hastily removed with a sharp knife. At one end of the house the winter storms have toppled a gable, which in falling has crushed the fragile camellia-house below; one surviving camellia blooms among the rubble of ironstone – the only flourishing vestige of Ecton's former splendour.

In 1989 an advertisement in *Country Life* magazine showed a smart, refurbished Ecton for sale as luxury apartments. Thus the period of emptiness and silence has come to an end. Perhaps the disinfectant quality of new paint and the presence of new fixtures and fittings may succeed in exorcizing the old curse, and maybe the lead will, this time, stay on the roof.

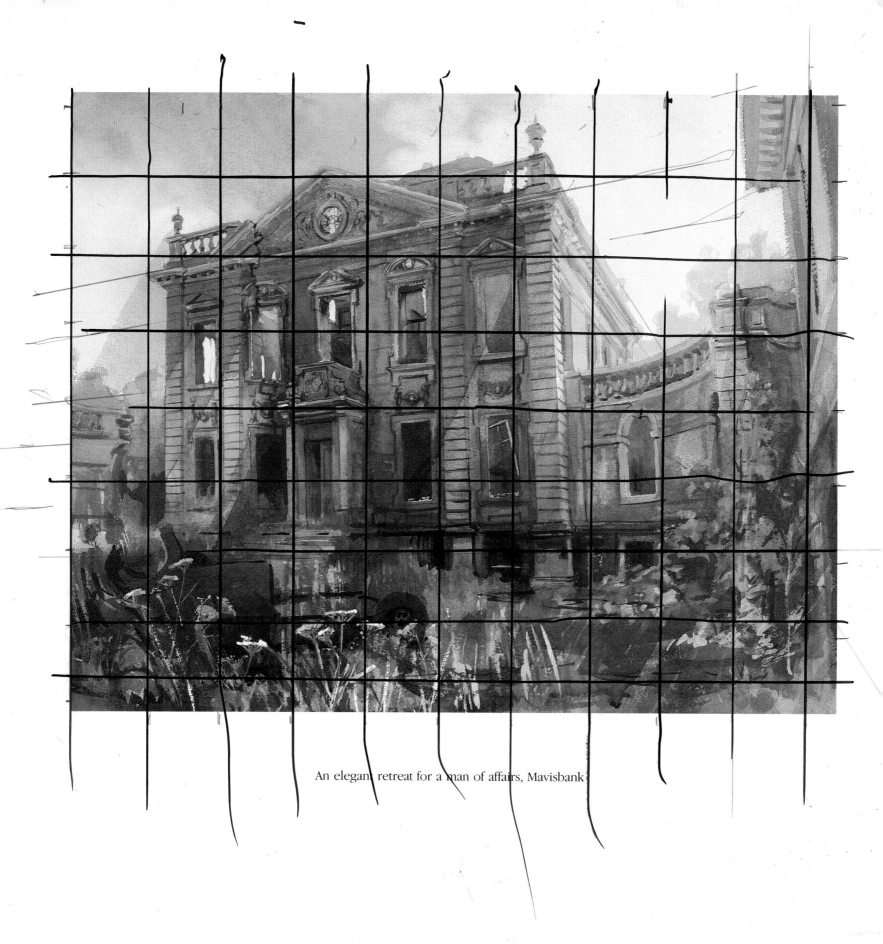

An elegant retreat for a man of affairs, Mavisbank

MAVISBANK HOUSE

Midlothian   Category A

On a wet autumn night in 1973 the Edinburgh fire brigade was called out to a secluded park to the south of the city, in answer to a confused call from Mavisbank. Its owner had retired to bed, very much the worse for drink, and had a last cigarette before going to sleep. When the fire engines arrived the whole house was engulfed by flames; the man had pulled himself and a few belongings out of the house before the fire had got a hold, but Mavisbank was gutted.

Many years later, workmen employed to shore up the crumbling shell of the house were clearing out debris from the cellar and were surprised by what they found inside. Since the fire the house had been used as a tip for old scrap iron – bits of motor cars and old washing machines filled the basement – and the floors had all fallen in, but there was a singular lack of any charred or burnt wood. There was no evidence of fixtures or fittings, no fireplaces or doorcases. Their suspicion grew with the discovery of metal pipes poking out of the basement walls, twisted and distorted by intense heat. The fire was supposed to have started in an upstairs bedroom, but this indicated that it had been at its most intense in the basement. No investigation was carried out at the time and the house just sat and rotted.

Mavisbank was built in 1723, designed by its owner, Sir John Clerk of Penicuik. Known as the 'Old Baron', in reverence to his position in the office of the Exchequer after the Union with England, Sir John was evidently a learned and charming man, as well as an aesthete and accomplished musician. His memoirs sparkle with wit and liberal ideas; in one incident he describes a cousin, one Alexander Clerk, who went for a walk one morning while his porridge cooled, and disappeared. Many years later he returned and calmly walked back into the house, just as if nothing had happened – he had been to Italy!

It was Sir John's own grand tour to Italy that had inspired him to leave the mark of his generation on the architecture of the day. With a strong respect for the family house at Penicuik, Sir John decided to build a new house nearby. His enthusiasm for the architecture of Ancient Rome, and his consequent disdain for the 'stony hallelujahs' of Vanbrugh, inspired him to draw up plans for a compact villa, an elegant retreat for a man of affairs. His amateur designs were adapted and put

The ruined façade of Mavisbank – a drawing

into a coherent and accurate form by William Adam, leading exponent of Georgian architecture in Scotland, and father of the great Robert Adam. In a poem, Sir John Clerk described Mavisbank:

> *". . . a little villa where one may*
> *Taste every Minutes Blessing Sweet and gay,*
> *and in a soft Retirement Spend the Day."*

Even now, in its gloomy and dilapidated state, Mavisbank is a gem, both charming and shocking at first sight. Surprisingly it is a small house, the richly-carved and decorated façade belying the scale. In the matter of decoration Sir John Clerk let his Baroque heart rule his Palladian head. To the sides, curved wings lead to two large pavilions that ironically gave Sir John some satisfaction that, 'in the event of a fire the entire house would not be destroyed – two of the three parts remaining that the family may safely retire into them'.

Mavisbank was sold in 1763 by Sir James Clerk after his father's death, and in 1815 it was sold again. Considerable neo-Greek additions were made at this time, filling out the areas between the main block and wings, and augmenting the flamboyant detailing. In 1876 it was acquired by the so-called 'Mavisbank Company', which ran it as a lunatic asylum. When the National Health Service was set up in 1948, the asylum was closed and the house bought by its last superintendent, Dr Harrowes, who began to restore it to the original Adam concept. However, costs overran and, despite grant-aid, work stopped. It was subsequently sold to a Mr Stevenson, whose previous house, Hatton in West Lothian, had burned down.

Regardless of the conjecture surrounding the fire on that autumn night, Mavisbank now has a strangely forbidding character. It glowers unhappily across its valley with a great scar running down its face; mining activities far beneath the foundations have forced a jagged crack from pediment to basement, one half sunk six inches lower than the other. In contrast to its eerie demeanour, Mavisbank has collected many friends in its struggle to survive. When it was threatened with demolition, these friends manifested themselves as a human blockade against the contractor's bulldozers until an alternative was found. Now the Lothian Building Preservation Trust has shored up the shell to hold it together until a new future can be established for this wonderful Baroque doll's house.

Mavisbank – a colour note

The walls still standing, Penicuik

PENICUIK HOUSE

Midlothian Category A

Sir John Clerk had built Mavisbank to satisfy his creative instincts, having returned from the Grand Tour brimming with visions of the Classical architecture of Europe, and his son would do the same at Penicuik. The young James followed in his father's footsteps around Europe, and returning to Penicuik, or Newbigging as it was then, he hid a certain disappointment with the rambling Jacobean towers and blocks of the house his grandfather had bought a century before. After the 'Old Baron's' death in 1755, Sir James set about designing and masterminding the construction of a substantial Neo-Classical mansion in its place. So the Clerk passion for building bore fruit into another generation.

The Penicuik estate has been owned by an unbroken line of Clerks since 1654, and the new house was a strong nucleus. In the middle of the 19th century the house was extended, with the addition of more bedrooms for Victorian house-parties. But tragically the house caught fire on June 16, 1899. The butler, returning to Penicuik to serve lunch, was the first to notice the fire; four fire engines were summoned immediately, but by the time they arrived the fire had already gained too strong a hold. It became clear the house itself could not be saved and all hands turned to rescuing the contents, piling them up on the front lawn.

At the time the house had been rented to an Edinburgh lawyer, and on hearing about the fire, Lady Clerk, wife of the eighth Baronet, at once came north to inspect the damage. A formidable figure, she immediately put in hand alterations to the stables, to make them habitable for the time being. Later it seemed as though the house could be rebuilt, but the insurance company refused to pay the full sum for which the house had been covered, on the grounds that the walls were still standing. So the family moved into the stable block, where they continue to live today, surrounded by the furniture, doorcases and fireplaces salvaged from the main house.

The ruin of Penicuik now stands like a vast austere folly surrounded by a gentle melancholy. It is as much a monument to the age that created it as it would have been had it not burnt down. The great portico that once served as 'a retreat from the inclemency of the weather ... and prevents the rain and the snow from beating into your house by the principal door', is now open to the clouds, and the door is gone.

A substantial Neo-Classical mansion, Penicuik

Above: Mottled light on the drive, Penicuik

Opposite: The broken balustrade in the portico, Penicuik

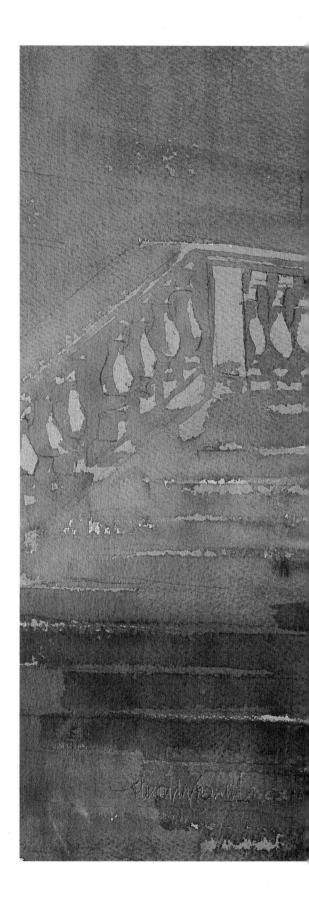

The house hidden in the trees, Pell Wall

PELL WALL HALL

Shropshire   Grade II*

Sir John Soane is often referred to as Britain's most original architect, an illustrious and idiosyncratic genius. Unfortunately very little of his work survives today. Of his country houses, several have been demolished and both Piercefield House and Pell Wall stand derelict. Of Pell Wall Soane wrote:

> *"In composing the plans of this villa my best energies have been exerted, intending that, when it was completed, my private professional labours should cease."*

It was for Soane's friend Purney Sillitoe that Pell Wall was designed, in 1822. By 1880 it had been sold to James Walker, of the whisky family, and many alterations were carried out, notably the addition of a new wing, sympathetic to Soane's design and containing an early example of an indoor swimming pool.

It was no act of fate that was responsible for Pell Wall's lengthy interval of dereliction. Until 1964 the house had served as a school, but was then bought by a man whose interest lay purely in the development possibilities of its site, which stands close to the bustling town of Market Drayton. The new owner promptly applied twice for permission to demolish the house, and was both times refused.

During the subsequent years the house deteriorated rapidly, probably encouraged by its owner? Vandalism and theft had also taken their toll, and in 1984 the local planning office received an application to carry out a 'controlled burning' of the interior. This ridiculous request was refused out of hand, and in 1985 the owner applied for a third time for consent to demolish, which was also refused.

Despite the rapid deterioration, the British Historic Buildings Trust has been trying to acquire what was left of Pell Wall, and had plans to completely restore it. The house was suffering badly from wilful neglect; the roof leaked, ceilings were falling down, and the local vandals had broken what they could. Anything of value had been stolen, but still the Trust tried everything to force the owner to sell.

With an impending compulsory purchase order from the council, it

The twisted balustrade, Pell Wall

was hardly surprising that in early 1986 a fire reduced Pell Wall to little more than a tottering shell. The saga of Pell Wall Hall had attracted much publicity, and by coincidence a television crew were on hand to witness the fire. However, when they tracked down the elusive owner to bring him the sad news, they found him neither sad nor at all keen to discuss the matter!

It was shortly after the fire that I first visited Pell Wall; the drive was heavily overgrown and the house completely hidden in the trees – it was only by bumping into the front steps that I found it. The front door stood open revealing the hall piled high with great blackened rafters and rubble. Further in, the marble staircase stood hidden under charred wood, and twisted iron was all that remained of the once-elegant balustrade. The central atrium of the house was open to the sky, bright, like a glade in a dismal wood, and infected with the foul stench of a burnt-out fire.

During the following winter I returned to Pell Wall; the trees without leaves no longer hiding the grey shell, which stood in bold contrast to the fresh powdering of snow. The familiar rubble within looked odd and the acrid aggression was now softened into a gentle silence – I had never seen snow *inside* a house before! The marble columns stood proud in their new landscape, and Pell Wall seemed calm and dreamy. But as I sketched the snow slowly melted, gradually revealing the sordid decay once again.

The façade cleared of trees, Pell Wall

Opposite: Marble columns in a snowy landscape, Pell Wall

PIERCEFIELD HOUSE

Monmouthshire   Grade II

Although Piercefield has been unoccupied since the late 1920s, it was hastened into dereliction by troops during the War. While encamped in the park, a battalion of American artillery used the façade of the house for target-practice, and the pock-marked stone still bears evidence against them. Originally the park was laid out in part by 'Capability' Brown, and it is now Chepstow Racecourse. The shell of the house, however, stands out of sight of the binoculars and forgotten.

A plan was put forward in 1982 to rebuild Piercefield as a vast hotel complex, incorporating only a token replica of the façade in concrete. But the plan foundered, leaving the fine front still staring out over the distant Severn estuary and the arc of the great bridge.

Piercefield, like Pell Wall, is a rare survivor from the drawing board of Sir John Soane, but both are in ruins. Uncluttered by frills and fashions, Piercefield's pure design is now perhaps more visible in its derelict state than if the varied tastes of wealthy owners and their interior designers had survived.

George Smith of County Durham bought the estate in 1784 for £26,000 and commissioned Soane to redesign the house, stipulating that part of the former Tudor house be incorporated at the back. However, Smith was bankrupted by the outbreak of the Napoleonic Wars ten years later and Piercefield was put up for sale at Christie's. It was bought by Lieutenant Colonel Mark Wood, MP, who engaged Joseph Bonomi to add the pavilions and a lavish interior. The hall was lined with Gobelin tapestries and access to the saloon was through great sliding doors, mirrored to reflect the wide view of the Severn. Now nothing remains, save two cast-iron scrolls that held up the gallery at the top of the stairs.

Over the 150 years following the departure of Bonomi, Piercefield was owned by eight different families, and it bankrupted three of them. Henry Hastings Clay, the last, sold the house and parkland to the Chepstow Racecourse Company in 1921. Naturally their interest was in the land, and the house slipped into decay. Approached through the park, the house stands in peaceful and majestic isolation, far from the drumming of hoofs while the rolling parkland descends to the gorge carved by the River Wye, and languishes like the Elysian fields of a Claude Lorraine landscape.

Opposite: The hall and saloon at Piercefield

Below: A Classical pavilion flanking the house, Piercefield

The portico at Bettisfield in the late afternoon

BETTISFIELD PARK

Flintshire   Grade II*

As one of the oldest families in north Wales, the Hanmers have owned the Bettisfield Estate since the 13th century. In later generations a tradition built up that each heir should add to the family house, to leave the mark of his era in the architecture fashionable at the time. Consequently, Bettisfield Park became a ridiculous pot-pourri of different architectural styles.

In the foundations lie the remains of a 16th-century house. Above stands the main block, a fine Regency mansion built, it is thought, by James Wyatt, and featuring fine interiors. In the early 1800s a stone portico and a vast Italianate campanile were added. A generation later saw the addition of a long Victorian wing, culminating in an even larger French tower, and various porches and bays appeared on the garden front as well as an assortment of augmentations for the service quarters at the rear. Thus the tradition continued, each new style ignorant of the others that preceded and followed it and each contributing to an overall architectural confusion.

By the Second World War the trend was thankfully reversed; the French tower and its vast wing were dismantled as the old Lord Hanmer concentrated only on his passion for racehorses. After the War he continued to live in the house, but its condition rapidly deteriorated and when the rain ran down the walls of the Green Drawing Room he moved to the West Drawing Room, and so on.

When the Lord died, the house was uninhabitable, and the interiors were sour with mould and dry-rot. The fabulous Greek-Revival plaster-work, painted ceilings and swagged friezes were crumbling. Once there were supposed to be frescos by Veronese and Zelotti, taken to Bettisfield from Venetian villas, but they had gone – all that was left in their place was a rich mould.

By 1990 the reversal was complete; the Hanmers sold the house and a restoration scheme was started, which involved the demolition of all the remaining Victorian bits and the Italian campanile. When the work had been completed only the original Regency mansion was left, free from its burdens; now the mouldy silence is broken, the plaster-work has been repainted and the slimy moss of the Green Drawing Room scraped off.

A dusty mirror and over-mantle in the hall, Bettisfield

Above: Sun through the windows of the Green Drawing Room, Bettisfield

Opposite: Greek-Revival plasterwork and swagged friezes, Bettisfield

BANK HALL

Lancashire   Grade II*

One of the houses I found most difficult to see was Bank Hall; the ivy-enshrouded shell stands in the centre of its estate, but a major road runs nearby, from which the tower and chimneys are just visible in the trees. Trouble in the past with vandals has imbued great vigilance in the gamekeeper and his family; he is now under firm orders to see off any uninvited visitors. Finally – and with permission – I arrived in front of the Hall during a snowstorm, the great black shape looming in the flurries, with a few pigeons darting for cover in its windows.

It is as the nucleus of a thriving estate that Bank Hall is so strongly defended, despite the fact that it is no longer inhabited. It was formerly the seat of the Lilfords, and the large agricultural estate-lands on the estuary of the River Ribble are still farmed by the family. Bank Hall was, and still is, its heart. It is a Jacobean brick mansion that dates back to 1608, with great curved gables and a high tower. These gables were repeated when the Hall was extended in 1832, to the designs of George Webster of Kendal. At the back of the house the tower contains the splintered remains of the early 17th-century staircase. This tower has now partially collapsed, a gaping wound that signals the death of the house. The body of the Hall is now clothed in thick robes of ivy – like Sleeping Beauty's castle – and snow settles in the hall; no beauty here, just an occasional creak from something stirring in the breeze.

During the War the house was used as a transit camp, and has been empty ever since. For a brief period part of it was used as the estate office, but by 1974 the dry rot had spread and it became unmanageable. Sad to see its decline, Lord Lilford obtained permission to dismantle the house and to re-use it to build a new Bank Hall. However, this work did not start at once, as it was thought better that a new house be built by a new generation; when the heir comes of age he will not only be in charge of the estates, but will also be encouraged to engage a worthy architect to design the new Hall.

Looking to that future, the present generation have planted copses and stands of beech and oak that will one day mature in the grounds of the new house. Perhaps the architect will keep the Jacobean tower, with its finials and clockfaces, so that future generations of Lilfords will be able to enjoy the views over the trees to the distant Irish Sea.

Opposite: The splintered remains of a 17th-century staircase, Bank Hall

Above: The greenhouse full of brambles, Bank Hall

Opposite: Bank Hall looming in the flurries of a
snowstorm

'The Watch-Tower of the Mountain', Gwylfa Hiraethog

GWYLFA HIRAETHOG

Denbighshire

On the very highest spot on the Denbigh Moors in north Wales, stands the extraordinary shell of Gwylfa Hiraethog, 'The Watch-Tower of the Mountain'. It was built as recently as 1913, as a shooting lodge for Lord Devonport. Originally there had been a log-cabin on the site, made in Norway and bolted to the rock to prevent it from blowing away – a wise precaution in the circumstances! It is its very position that has hastened a speedy decline and, more importantly, given Gwylfa its unique character.

The site on top of the moors is certainly striking; the second Lord Devonport relates how, as a child, he climbed by carriage the long steep miles from the station at Denbigh up to the house, and recalls the spectacular views from the top. Gwylfa is reputed to be the highest private house in Britain, and the Lord remembers seeing the Isle of Man, the Mourne mountains in Ulster and the distant Mull of Galloway in Scotland. On one exceptionally clear day, his father sent a telegram to a business associate who lived in the Mourne mountains, saying: "We can see you, can you see us?" His laconic colleague replied with a curt, "Yes ditto".

Today, climbing the steep road into snowy January skies, the desolation of Gwylfa is extreme. The silhouette on the skyline looms dark as a satanic mill, incongruous in its bleak tree-less surroundings. The contrast between the thin driven snow and the wet granite stones of the ruin is stark black and white. In 1925 Lord Devonport tried unsuccessfully to sell the house. With not a footprint in the snow, nor a tree to give shelter, it would be an exceptional person who would choose such a site for a home, and, not surprisingly, by the 1950s it was ruined. The fierce gales had systematically dismantled this substantial house that once dared to stand in their way.

With the reputation of being the highest house with the finest view in Britain, it is strange that Gwylfa also holds what must be another record: it appears to be the house to which vandals have made the greatest pilgrimage. Not only is it a ten-mile drive from the nearest town, but it is also a half-mile walk from the road below – a long way to carry a pot of paint and a brush with which to scrawl a name or two and an associated message!

Driven snow and wet granite, Gwylfa Hiraethog

Melton Constable

MELTON CONSTABLE

Norfolk   Grade I

Melton Constable was put up for sale in 1986 and acquired the accolade of 'the finest Grade I listed house in the country not presently occupied'. It had not actually been occupied for 40 years and stood forgotten in the flat Norfolk countryside. Ten years earlier it had achieved a certain fame as the location for Joseph Losey's film '*The Go-Between*', but since then it had sunk back into oblivion.

A fine house it certainly is, built between 1664 and 1687 in the style of Sir Christopher Wren. The partially rustic style of the detailing suggests that it is the work of the Norfolk architect Sir Roger Pratt. If so, it is unique as his other houses have been much altered over the centuries.

Melton Constable Hall stands majestically in 200 acres of parkland far from the nearest road, with a feeling that the Astley family, who built it, have just moved out. In fact, they sold the house just after the Second World War to the Duke of Westminster, who found it to be surplus to his needs and sold it on to a local farmer, in 1959, who worked the land and tended the gardens, but never lived in the house.

In 1986 the interior was exactly how the Astley's had left it; on the great staircase, huge family portraits hung blackened and limp in their frames, wall-paper and silk hangings in the morning room bowed graciously off the walls, and the dining room ceiling was implored by wooden crutches to cling to its rafters. Given the state of decay, the pristine condition of marble fireplaces and delicate Chinese wall-paper came as something of a surprise. In the drawing room a fine ceiling dripping with baroque fruit, flowers and game-birds – like a huge, plaster Grinling Gibbons – survived in all its exuberance.

Behind the green-baize door, the kitchens contained a crescendo of old mangles and radiators, and the oven doors stood open expectantly. The wine and silver vaults hosted only the spirit of grandeur, and among the dust and junk a little silver teaspoon glimmered in the darkness – such was the strength of the link with the past. Outside, great cedar trees gracefully stooped like aged dancers, and the walls of the kitchen garden restrained the riot of brambles inside. Visiting Melton Constable was like prying into the privacy of the Astleys, so complete was the house. It had the serenity and dignity of an elderly statesman, free from the vulgarity of division and refurbishment recommended by the estate agents.

A dried-up fountain on the front lawn, Melton Constable

ECCLESGRIEG HOUSE

Kincardineshire Category B

Ecclesgrieg is a surprising prospect viewed from the main coast road from Montrose to Aberdeen. At first sight it appears to be quite complete in its formal gardens; a late 19th-century house in the best Scottish Gothic style. Regardless of its appearance, however, it has in fact been empty for many years, yet structurally is perfectly sound.

On closer inspection the first hint of something unusual appears; instead of a car parked outside the front door, a large red grain lorry stands close to the house, and a shiny metal pipe protrudes from an upstairs window. There is an explanation for this somewhat surrealist vision, and it lies behind the windows of the ground floor rooms. The glass in the windows has been painted black on the inside, for within all the main rooms have been lined with corrugated iron. Ecclesgrieg is now a grain silo.

When the family ceased to live in the house, the Estate Company converted the entire carcass into a grain store; a chute loads the grain from a conveyor into the top of a turret, and it is then passed by conveyor into one of the main bins inside. When the grain is ready to be sold, another chute points out of a bedroom window into the big red truck – simple! Despite the removal of the floors and walls inside, necessity has dictated that the only surviving feature of the interior is the staircase, with its stained-glass window diffusing coloured light onto the dusty treads below. The grain bins fill the rest of the space, crammed in like balloons in a box.

As such, this may seem a peculiar use for a country house. However, grain must be kept dry, and so indeed must the fabric of a house. If nobody wants to live in the house then at least in this form it will be well-maintained. The roof is perfect and the windows weather-proof. In the winter months as the northeasterly gales bring driving rain from Scandinavia the driers maintain a constant temperature and a moisture-free environment. For the rodent population, Ecclesgrieg must be equivalent to a de-luxe hotel. To complete the disguise, the pretty Victorian garden, featuring balustrades and box parterres, is lovingly maintained by the local villagers. In the summer they use the lawn to play croquet, disturbed only by the rumble of the occasional lorry on its way to and from the house.

Above: The Victorian garden with its balustrade and parterres, Ecclesgrieg

Opposite: A stained-glass window diffusing coloured light onto dusty treads, Ecclesgrieg

The drive, no more than tractor tracks through a field, Urie House

URIE HOUSE

Kincardineshire   Category B

Some way further up the North Sea coast from Ecclesgrieg is a spectacular ruined shell, visible from afar, overlooking the river Cowie. A fine mansion in the Elizabethan style, Urie House was built in the Victorian era, the date 1855 appearing on a key-stone.

The Barclays of Ury (*sic*) are recorded as having taken the estate in 1647 and kept it until the death in 1853 of Captain R. Barclay-Allardyce. He became famous as a great pedestrian who established a record for walking a thousand miles in as many hours. The estate was then sold to Alexander Baird, a successful ironmaster from Gartsherrie, with hundreds of acres of finely-timbered grounds, including the whole river valley. Baird chose a bluff on a bend in the river as the site for his mansion, and built the new Urie – the largest house in the county.

From a distance the house today is certainly imposing, although the south front is completely obscured by saplings and a wing has collapsed. On close inspection the most striking aspect is the sheer scale of the design; the windows are tall, the rooms substantial and the *porte-cochère* belittling. The central tower soars to a great height above the trees, and once sported a grand banner. However, once inside the house past the cavernous entrance hall, the principal rooms are connected by a comparatively narrow passage that runs the length of the house. In the middle of this passage rise the stairs whose scale is positively diminutive. Evidently the gesture of grandeur was only to apply to those visitors who could be confined to the ground floor.

Whether the accommodation of the first floor was on a similar scale to the rooms below will never be known, as all the floors have fallen in, and the arc of the stone stairs is now severed, leading nowhere. Under the great *porte-cochère* great round straw bales now lie, and in front stands a silage heap covered in car tyres. The drive is no more than tractor tracks through a field, its puddles reflecting the noble silhouette in the evening light. In the garden, persistence through the dense saplings and brambles rewards with the discovery of a flight of stone steps that lead towards the ha-ha and fields. To one side a path descends steeply, created by an avalanche of masonry from part of the service wing that crumbled into the river. Recently the house was listed Category B, so perhaps no more of it will be allowed to fall into the river?

A flight of steps hidden in the garden, Urie House

Above: A spectacular ruined shell visible from afar, Urie House

Opposite: Stone stairs at Urie House that lead nowhere

The overgrown terraces of the Italian garden at Belladrum

BELLADRUM HOUSE

Inverness-shire

The history of Belladrum House and its domain may be characteristic of its type, but its future may be a precedent. The first estate at Belladrum was founded by a Fraser, a clan whose nucleus was Inverness. A fine Georgian house was built in the late 18th century, and substantial grounds laid out and nursed by Ninian Niven, whose treatises on viniculture were famous at the time. By the early 19th century, financial difficulties forced the son of Colonel James Fraser to sell the estate, and it was acquired by James Stuart. An extensive programme of rebuilding was started, its new owner anxious to make his mark among the country houses of Scotland, and to celebrate his great wealth gleaned from the plantations of the West Indies. The entire house was remodelled in the style of a French château. Stuart ordered vast quantities of the finest stone to be brought from nearby Elgin, and completed the Europeanization by laying a terraced Italianate garden to the west of the house.

But within 30 years Belladrum had again been sold; James Merry, ironmaster and railway pioneer, took Belladrum as his seat, and in so doing conceived a great engineering plan. Hitherto the only access to Inverness was by rail through Aberdeen. The dog-legged journey from Edinburgh irritated Merry, and as a result he conceived the present line that winds through the most mountainous regions of the Grampians, direct to Inverness.

By the end of the 19th century, Belladrum enjoyed a grand lifestyle – a glimpse of Parisian chic amidst the austere Scottish hills. However, Belladrum had been in the Merry family for exactly 100 years when in 1957 Ian Merry demolished the house. In the same year his grandson was born, and it is he who now carries the Belladrum banner. The family retreated to the estate factor's house, and after the death of Ian Merry his daughter sold the entire estate to a Dutchman, who broke it up it into multiple ownership.

Yet, in 1987 the factor's house was bought back into the family, as were the overgrown Italian gardens a year later. Now James Merry's railway line carries his descendant back to Belladrum, and one day a new house will be built overlooking the terraces and replanted beds of the Italian garden.

Lupins run wild at Belladrum

The 1200-year-old 'Yew of Loudon'

LOUDON CASTLE

Ayrshire   Category B

Once termed 'the Windsor of Scotland', Loudon Castle has stood as an empty shell since it was gutted by fire in 1941. It is a great fortress of a house, with square towers and battlements; a true sham castle. Archibald Elliot, an Edinburgh architect who specialized in castellated country houses with gothic detailing, was commissioned in 1804 to build the castle for the Countess of Loudon, wife of the second Earl of Moira. His grandiose design was to incorporate the remains of a 15th-century keep, the previous Loudon Castle, and later 17th-century work. The finished castle owed much in concept to the work of Robert Adam, notably the latter's romantic Dalquharran Castle on the Ayrshire coast.

Loudon stands on a hillside overlooking the river Irvine, its jagged crenellated outline visible from miles away. The drive leads up a long avenue of mature trees, around a circular lawn and up twin ramps to the front door. The lawn is mown and the drive still used by the owners who live in a new house nearby, the ruins of the castle making an extraordinary folly in their garden.

During the fire of '41 a great deal of the interior was destroyed, including a large and valuable library for which the castle was famous. Mercifully, however, a great yew tree alongside the castle survived the fire. It lives today, almost obliterating the massive south façade of the castle. 'The old yew of Loudon' is reputed to be 1200 years old, its trunk of an enormous diameter hidden under the spreading boughs. It was the custom to sign important documents under its canopy, and it is said that the third Earl of Loudon signed the treaty of Union with England in its shade in 1705 – an unsubstantiated story, perhaps promulgated by those who opposed the Union and thought it appropriate that such a treaty should be signed in the deep shadow so conveniently available to the Earl, who was in part responsible for its terms.

Loudon would cost so much to restore today that the only future for it is as a romantic ruin. Its long avenue of mature trees is now the drive to a new bungalow, the inhabitants of which are able to enjoy this fantastic folly as it gradually and inevitably falls down in front of them. If the old yew survives it will have witnessed the birth, heyday and demise of two castles on the site; perhaps if it lives long enough it will witness the creation of a third?

'The Windsor of Scotland', Loudon Castle

The Great Hall with its brace and hammer-beam roof, Vale Royal Abbey

VALE ROYAL ABBEY

Cheshire   Grade II

The great, rambling Victorian structure of Vale Royal Abbey disguises well its medieval origins, only its name suggesting anything of its history. But within the clumsy exterior lie the remains of a Cistercian monastery. Edward I's men had scoured England searching for a suitable site for the monastery, which eventually they found on the banks of the river Weaver. A great abbey was built together with the largest Cistercian church in the land, and it thrived for three centuries. A local legend relates how, during this time, a beautiful nun was caught '*in flagrante*' with a monk, as a result of which she was buried alive in the monastery, and recently her little stone coffin was found in the undergrowth.

In 1543 Henry VIII's dissolution of the monasteries ended the life of the abbey and the great church was pulled down, its stones used by Thomas Holcroft who had acquired the site. With them he built a great house around the former halls and cloisters. Now only a vandalized monument marks the position of the altar, but the cloisters, abbot's hall and refectory are to be found deep inside the newer house, and sometimes the figure of a nun is seen flitting through the abandoned rooms.

The rambling structure of Vale Royal Abbey

In 1616 Vale Royal became the home of the Cholmondeley family, and over the generations they altered the house considerably. The great abbot's hall became three substantial rooms: the Armoury, the Great Hall, with its brace and hammer-beam roof, and the Library. In later Victorian times they added a new façade, giving the Abbey its present severe aspect. The Cholmondeleys lived at Vale Royal until it was requisitioned in 1939, and after the War it was sold to ICI to provide accommodation for their Polish employees. Unfortunately most of the valuable heraldic fittings were sold off.

By 1977 Vale Royal had become surplus to the requirements of ICI, and was bought by a charitable trust who used labour from the Manpower Services in a bodged attempt to restore the building. But the work soon stopped and the house was again sold, beginning a period of complete desolation and a multitude of owners. One night someone set fire to a caravan belonging to a firm of dry-rot specialists working on site. The lads inside escaped, but their dog died. Now on gloomy nights, a little dog is sometimes heard barking inside the empty mansion.

Ash trees in the Great Banqueting Hall of Ruperra

RUPERRA CASTLE

Mid Glamorgan   Grade II*   Scheduled Ancient Monument

The ruins of Ruperra Castle stand as a stout sham castle – a great four-square crenellated block with round towers at the corners. Four storeys high and roofless, its former whitewashed exterior is now a gloomy grey stucco hatched with cracks. During a gale in 1982 one of the towers split from top to bottom, the outer half falling out onto the lawn, scattering a long line of stone down the garden. The standing half is like the bleeding stump of a severed limb – a comparison heightened by the gory colour of the internal brickwork, now exposed in contrast to the grey stucco.

The royal coat of arms, Ruperra – a sketch

The building of Ruperra was completed in 1626, its fortress design derived from Medieval defensive architecture but translated into Renaissance domestic. Its strong similarity to the coeval Lulworth Castle in Dorset has given rise to uncertainty as to its architect – some reports favour Robert Smythson, others Inigo Jones. Either way, its importance as a building has earned it the title of a Scheduled Monument, a designation that may yet preserve it. To see the shell across the fields in the hills above Cardiff leaves one in no doubt as to its significance.

It was built for Sir Thomas Morgan, steward to the Earl of Pembroke, and Charles I stayed there for two days in 1645 after the Battle of Naseby. His visit is commemorated in the royal coat of arms above the south porch. Despite a bad fire in 1785 the castle has survived unaltered, save for a new Victorian porch on the east front and the crenellated roofline that replaced earlier gables.

The castle passed through the Morgan family, later the Viscounts Tredegar, and became principally a house for the elder sons before they inherited the nearby Tredegar estate. In the 1920s the last heir, Courtney Morgan, succeeded to Tredegar, and Ruperra subsequently was kept for house parties and shoots. In April of 1935 the house and contents were put up for sale. While the furniture was sold, the castle was unwanted and abandoned – its fine gardens left to go wild, the team of 13 gardeners laid off.

Six years later Dutch troops were billeted in the empty house, and on the 6th of December – the night of the Japanese bombing of Pearl Harbour – a fire broke out. Some say it had been started deliberately by the unhappy troops who had hoped to be transferred. All they achieved was a transfer to spartan huts on the lawn. The fire raged through the oak-panelled interior and blazed like a great beacon, visible from Newport and Cardiff. The fire engines had got stuck in the narrow lanes, and by dawn it was wrecked.

The ruin and its domain were sold for a pathetic £16,000 to a local farmer, and there it stands, slowly falling down. But developers have been seen sniffing around the park, and plans are in the air for restoration. Sadly, 'restoration' in this case involves merely using the shell to clothe a block of flats, and the construction of a housing estate in the garden, as Newport rapidly edges closer. If the ruin is indeed re-used, like nearby Tredegar, it will be surrounded by a sprawl of superstores, car parks and modern offices in the style of the Carolean 'word-processor' vernacular. Such development would be so insulting that it might be kinder to let it fall down completely – a path it is already on.

Despite the apparent solidity of the castle, on three of its four corners, ominous cracks widen within. The 17th-century brickwork is loosening its grip and the weather is forcing it apart. In the Great Banqueting Hall, which was once panelled and hung with arms and armour, a small copse of ash trees has grown up, their trunks thick and straight as the branches reach for the sky three storeys above. Below the rubble floor their roots wrestle with the foundations, growing stronger with every season.

Opposite: The royal coat of arms above the south porch of Ruperra

One of the towers split from top to bottom, Ruperra

Salmon-pink brickwork and whitewash, Pickhill

PICKHILL HALL

Flintshire   Grade II

Pickhill Hall was familiar to me from two contrasting photographs; the one showed its cheerful countenance overlooking a tidy lawn, a delicate conservatory to one side and its windows open to let in the summer air. In the second the lawn was an unkempt meadow and the façade marred by broken windows and brambles. The roof was a framework of blackened rafters, and the conservatory replaced by a clumsy corrugated-iron shed. The two pictures covered a period of some 20 years and told a sad tale.

The house stands a few safe feet above the flood-plains of the river Dee in the Welsh Marches. It is a charming Queen Anne façade, bright in contrast between the salmon-pink brickwork and the whitewash of the carved-stone dressings. It is Baroque in its detailing and attributed to the work of Richard Trubshaw in or around 1720. It is unique in Wales and to the untrained eye it bears a close resemblance to the work of Francis Smith of Warwick, and in particular to Buntingsdale Hall, just over the border in Shropshire.

In both cases the period of emptiness and silence has come to an end, but the causes were very different. At Buntingsdale the family had been deprived of their home by the needs of the armed forces during the War, but at Pickhill its family had deprived themselves. After the War they moved out of the house, and used it only occasionally to hold a ball or function. Consequently it was sparsely furnished and not looked after. Faced with pressure from the authorities, the family found themselves unable to do anything constructive with the house, and rather than sell it they set fire to it.

The second photograph had illustrated its demise to the authorities who were concerned for its future, and after three years a buyer succeeded in persuading the owners to sell it. Nothing remained of the interiors and the structure was beginning to collapse, but the new owner reversed the process of decay. Plans were agreed and work started on the task of converting it into so-called 'units'. Here the similarity with Buntingsdale surfaces again, as one of these has been bought by a descendant of the original family that owned Pickhill, some 150 years ago. In place of the corrugated-iron shed now stands a fine new conservatory.

The open door and rubble within, Pickhill

Weeds and flowers on the front steps, Buntingsdale

BUNTINGSDALE HALL

Shropshire   Grade II*

In 1988 Market Drayton witnessed a great commotion and shuffling of papers in council planning circles, as public inquiries and bureaucratic machinations attempted to save Pell Wall Hall. But on the other side of the town Buntingsdale Hall stood as a monument to ill-conceived development, its demise continuing in a complex tangle of legal conundrums.

Built in 1721 by Francis Smith of Warwick for Bulkeley Mackworth, whose initials 'B M' appear on the straps securing the rain-water heads, the house was 'picturesquely bosomed in trees' until the Second World War. Buntingsdale is considered to be without question one of Smith's most original designs. Both the garden and entrance fronts are of identical Baroque design, rising to three storeys of precise brickwork and carved stone pilasters. In 1857 an extension was added at one side, with a fine ballroom and additional rooms upstairs. This was designed by another Mr Smith who, although no relation, sensitively maintained the style established by his namesake and predecessor.

The Mackworth family, and then their cousins, continued to live at Buntingsdale right up until the Second World War, when it was taken over as the Officers' Headquarters of the RAF No 10 Flying Training School. In the hands of the Ministry of Defence the house was well maintained, but by 1980 it had become surplus to requirements and was offered for sale.

Buntingsdale was bought by developers, and with the motivation of a fast profit, work was started on converting the house into flats, but in conflict with conservation guidelines – a drunk might have performed heart surgery more sensitively; stairways were cut through cornices and windows made into doorways, while internal doors were sealed, upsetting the symmetry and wrecking the principal rooms.

Suddenly work stopped. Something had gone wrong. The lead was removed from the roof, some of the overmantles and carved doorcases were hastily ripped out and the developers disappeared. Some of the units had already been sold, a building society foreclosed on one buyer and the creditors arrived on the doorstep. This left Buntingsdale in irons; anyone with a *bona-fide* restoration plan would first have to sort out a cat's-cradle of multiple ownership.

The lantern on the steps, Buntingsdale

Yet help was at hand; over the gloomy horizon appeared a brave new Mackworth, a descendant of the 'BM' on the rain-heads, who succeeded in buying one end of the house. In his part the roof has been repaired, the rot extinguished and the dark Victorian panelling whitewashed. Elsewhere, all that can be done in the meantime is to laboriously shuffle buckets under the drips, and to search for a way to disentangle the cat's-cradle.

As I sketched in the dining-room, one of the shutters swung away from its casement revealing a secret door with a recessed catch; each window had one, as the elderly caretaker demonstrated with a twinkle in his eye – "you see, in the old days when the ladies retired after dinner," he confided, "the gentlemen settled into their port and wouldn't be bothered with going to the loo to relieve themselves". The secret cupboards originally hid a selection of chamber-pots – the epitome of decadent convenience.

Three storeys of precise brickwork and carved stone pilasters, Buntingsdale

Buntingsdale Hall

The door to the entrance hall, Buntingsdale

'There was a crooked man who had a crooked house', Sinai Park

SINAI PARK

Staffordshire   Grade II*

Sinai Park is the oldest house in this collection, and the only timber building that has survived in a derelict condition for 30 years. For a pre-Reformation house its position is extraordinarily exposed – monasteries, gentry houses and other non-defensive buildings were usually built in the seclusion of a valley, protected from the elements and close to a water-source, as was Sinai's parent, the Benedictine monastery far below at Burton-upon-Trent. Of course, with a name like 'Sinai' it had to have religious roots, and indeed reference to the hallowed Mount makes its position on top of a hill a little less surprising.

The greater part of the house was originally a summer residence for the abbots of Burton, and before that its site is thought to have been a Roman hill fort; with views to all points of the compass it would certainly have been an ideal defensive position. High in their commanding eyrie the abbots ruled Sinai until Henry VIII dissolved their monastery and gave the house to his friend and executor, Sir William Paget. As the first Marquis of Anglesey, Paget spent a brief period at Sinai, and evidently entertained lavishly during that time.

Thus after the Reformation, Sinai continued to exist as a house, a large U-shaped, timber-framed mansion. It was altered a little in the 17th century, but by the 19th it had fallen on hard times. Although the ancient timbers had survived well, by the turn of the 20th century brick additions had been tacked on, and scruffy repairs made. It was subsequently split into three farm-workers' dwellings, but with the whole house now encased in stucco the wood suffocated in what had become an ideal environment for the spores of rot to flourish – just like the dark damp shelves of a mushroom farm. As parts of the house weakened and broke, so it began to tilt and cant into a caricature, the stucco flaking off and revealing the rotten bones beneath. The first floor overhung the lower, giving it a top-heavy look, so in little time it became reminiscent of a fairy-story . . . '*there was a crooked man who had a crooked house . . .*', as it sagged and bowed.

By the 1960s it was empty, the interior fittings removed and parts of the house used as a pig-shed. Now, however, 20th-century carpenters put into practice what they have learnt from their Tudor counterparts – Sinai Park is being restored!

A pair of wrought-iron gates hanging drunkenly from the
gateposts, Aberpergwm

ABERPERGWM HOUSE

West Glamorgan   Grade II

Surrounded on all sides by the mighty Brecon Beacons, Aberpergwm House would once have been sheltered in splendid isolation in the valley, but its tranquillity is now shattered by a noisy housing estate and the grinding clamour of an active coal mine. Near the road where great lorries rumble ceaselessly by, a pair of wrought-iron gates hang drunkenly from the gateposts, lurching in the breeze. At the top of the drive, the façade of the house also appeared to move – one gable had fallen in, and the next sloped inward at a surreal angle.

The original house was medieval, then known as Neuadd Pergwm, and became a centre of bardic patronage, playing host to poets and writers. It was inhabited throughout four centuries by the Williams family, who had inherited a lease of the former monastic lands in the valley. The present house is a 19th-century remodelling of the earlier building, and appears as a pretty country house in a pre-war photograph. It was used in the 1950s by the National Coal Board as offices, while they mined in the park, but since then, despite attempts to find alternative uses, the house has remained empty. With fundamental structural problems, such as walls that can no longer support each other, Aberpergwm cannot last much longer.

A year on, the valley looked the same – its sprawl of grey houses, grimy from the mine, bustled with Lowry figures as a shift changed and children came home from school. Snow-laden clouds hung overhead and dirty puddles covered the roads. But at Aberpergwm another winter had changed a lot; access to the house was unhindered now as the fine wrought-iron gates had gone, doubtless to turn up one day in the catalogue of a specialist in architectural reclamation.

In the garden a huge monkey-puzzle tree had fallen in a gale, and as the wind had funnelled up the valley, so the entire façade of the house had toppled over backwards into a growing heap of rubble. Curiously only the front door remained, flanked by several windows, and through its broken panels slid little pieces of masonry disturbed by a squirrel darting about on top of what had once been a house.

So the earlier prediction had come true sooner than expected, and in a matter of a short time now, Aberpergwm will be little more than a name on an old map.

The front door at Aberpergwm

WOODCHESTER PARK

Gloucestershire   Grade I

Whether fashionable or not, the sight of a Victorian interior preserved in its entirety is a salutary lesson to those who believe that building means putting something up cheaply, and never mind how long it lasts; at Yeaton Pevery in Shropshire, for example, the interior is remarkably intact, even though it was last occupied 15 years ago. Woodchester is extraordinary, however, as not only was it never occupied, it was never even finished!

The seclusion of a deep verdant valley has isolated the fabric of Woodchester from the attentions of thieves and vandals, and has ensured that it has survived the 120 years since the builders left. A mile walk through a wood pungently carpeted with wild garlic, across a scruffy meadow and there you are – a long way from the bustle of the 20th century. Seen from the outside the mansion is a good hefty chunk of High-Victorian Gothic; stone roof, stone mullions, macabre stone gargoyles, even stone gutters and down-pipes – not dreary grey stone, however, but the most delicious honey limestone, beautifully worked.

The greatest surprise of all comes inside the house. In the hall the floor is earth, the walls are bare rough-hewn stone and three fireplaces rise to the massive roof-joists 50 feet above. In the corners are springing points, awaiting their burden of stone vaulting. In the drawing room the rib-vaults are complete, but the windows unglazed and the walls unplastered. In the dining room a wooden scaffold still supports a brick arch, and a ladder leans to one side. In the chapel, the most magnificent room in the building, the carving is complete – beautiful – but there is no floor. Something happened 120 years ago, and the builders left in a tearing hurry.

All over the house the signs of this urgent departure are evident; a stone gargoyle lies unfinished on the floor, some walls are plastered, some left bare, and various tools are lying about. The theories are diverse. The house was built for William Leith by an architect in his early twenties, Benjamin Bucknall. Leith was a wealthy pious convert to Catholicism, devoted to the creation of monastic institutions and the upholding of his religious fervour. The young Bucknall was a keen admirer of the French theorist, Eugène Viollet-le-Duc, and this project presented him with the perfect opportunity to put the master's theories

Opposite: Stone fireplaces at Woodchester

into practice, and he designed a small-scale monastery, complete with a chapel and sacristy, as well as a brewery, bakery and cheese-room – monasticism extended even to separate male and female staff staircases.

The combination of enthusiastic architect and excellent masons produced this unique demonstration of Victorian craftsmanship. As outside, virtually everything inside is made of stone; there is a stone bath with stone spouts as taps, a stone shower – an extraordinary luxury for the 1850s – stone waste pipes and so on. The precision of the work is such that one could not even force a knife blade between the stones.

However, one must ask why did such excellent work suddenly stop? Some say that there was a murder in the house, while others believe that Leith had 'an experience' and lost the urge to live there. And some say that he simply ran out of money, and retired to his 16-bedroomed 'cottage', as it was called, that stood nearby.

Woodchester will remain a mystery, but the fabric of the house is to be preserved as a living museum of the Victorian art of building. It was reported that a visiting estate agent excitedly calculated the value of the stone at half-a-million pounds – a quarter of a million in demolition costs and a quarter of a million profit. Regardless of taste, the discovery and analysis of such workmanship will stop anyone making that sort of calculation again, and might demonstrate to some exactly what excellence means.

Opposite: The windows unglazed and walls unplastered, Woodchester

The house and chapel windows from the east, Woodchester

Sunlight through the mullion windows, Gibside

GIBSIDE

County Durham   Grade II*

The estate of Gibside, with its 17th-century Jacobean mansion passed by marriage from the Blakiston to the Bowes family in the 1720s. Sir George Bowes then added a north wing in the same style and designed a a unique landscaped setting for the house. At one end of an avenue of oaks he placed a startlingly-high column, topped with a statue of British Liberty, and at the other end, a mile away, he began to build a chapel designed by James Paine, thought to be the most outstanding Georgian building in the North East. By the time it was finished, two generations and a sad period for the family had passed.

Sir George Bowes' only child, Mary Eleanor inherited the estate, then valued at over a million pounds, in 1760 and married John Lyon, ninth Earl of Strathmore. After nine years and five children, the Earl died and Mary Eleanor found herself the object of the attentions of an attractive, but thoroughly poisonous Irish fortune-hunter by the name of Captain Stoney. He lured her into marriage, less than a year after the Earl's death, and then worked his way through her fortune, violently imprisoning her in Gibside and forbidding her even to see her children. Eventually, she was so terrified that she sought the protection of the law in London, and filed for divorce. Undeterred, Stoney Bowes abducted her, taking her on a terrible headlong coach chase to Northumberland, where she was finally rescued. Bowes was locked up for the rest of his life, but the 'Unhappy Countess' never returned to Gibside.

The estate was inherited by her eldest son, a mild man, and for a while the future of Gibside looked happier. However, a great scandal developed when he fell in love with Lady Tyrconnel, whose untimely death at the house gave away their secret to all. The day before the Earl died he married his mistress, Mary Millner, who had borne him a son; heir to the estate but not the title, John Bowes had no great interest in Gibside, preferring to live in Paris with his French wife, and later at nearby Barnard Castle where he built the Bowes Museum. But the Bowes fortunes from coal and steel were waning, and by the First World War Gibside was empty.

The future of the house now remains bleak; large trees grow in its roofless shell, their roots disturbing the foundations, and in the valley, modern Newcastle creeps ever closer.

A detail of the coat of arms over the front door, Gibside

CAMS HALL

Hampshire   Grade II

Some way eastwards along the coast from Highcliffe Castle there is another shell, through the empty windows of which the sea breezes constantly drift. Cams Hall, and its home farm, stand on a wide promontory at the head of Fareham Creek. From the terrace the view stretches down to Gosport and Portsmouth – provided the air is clear enough, it is just possible to make out the masts of HMS Victory in her dry dock amid the grey towers of today's Royal Navy. But the Hall has been left behind in the rush to develop this strategically important area, and now stands somewhat forlornly like the hulk of a shipwreck at low tide, surrounded by a sea of grass.

The Hall was an early 18th-century development of a 17th-century house, and when it was sold by General Carnac to John Delmé, it was again remodelled, in 1771, to the designs of Jacob Leroux. Delmé added the present Classical façade to the north front and two wings to the east and west. One contains various service quarters, but the other is purely a sham. Delmé died before the alterations were complete but his family lived on in the Hall, and legend has it that Emma Hamilton stayed there for a while to be closer to her beloved Nelson.

As a seaside retreat, the house itself consists of a small central block, with a large apse on the south side that once provided three storeys of sunny rooms, topped by a belvedere on the roof. Now, however, the intervening floors have gone and all three storeys are one. As long ago as 1956 the Hall was in a sorry state; an old photograph shows the windows shuttered, the stucco peeling and an old Morris parked outside. By the 1980s the façade was engulfed with ivy and the roof had collapsed, all its lead stolen. By 1990 the whole building was shored up with a framework of scaffolding, its guts lying in a heap on the front lawn as developers embarked on the first stages of restoration.

Behind its cobweb of pipes and clamps the house retains little of the charm that once graced its light and airy apartments; fragments of marble column, plaster cornice and cast-iron balustrade having been ground into the mud underfoot. And as restoration work proceeds, so the view to the south will close up as a forest of modern housing grows up in what was once the park. Thus, irreversibly, the 20th century is catching up with Cams Hall at last.

Opposite: Three storeys of stairs, Cams Hall

CAMS HALL

Above: A framework of scaffolding around Cams Hall

Opposite: Fragments of marble column and plaster cornice, Cams Hall

A mottled radiance over the ashen stone of House of Gray

HOUSE OF GRAY

Angus   Category A

From the front steps of the House of Gray a wide panorama opens up to the south beneath a busy autumn sky; to the left the tower-blocks of modern Dundee march around the corner, like a giant army gobbling up the countryside. Directly in front lie acres of gentle rolling fields descending to the silvery ribbon of the Firth of Tay. Beyond, the hills of Fife shimmer blue in the distant sun. To the immediate right an ancient cedar of Lebanon stoops over the west pavilion of the house, like an old statesman bending to hear the words of a child.

Such was the site chosen in 1715 by the tenth Lord Gray for his new mansion. It was built to the designs of William Adam (who later helped to design Mavisbank) and is one of the finest examples of Palladian architecture in Scotland. Broad steps lead up to the front door on the south side, an elegant façade flanked by two low pavilions. Set slightly back are two square staircase towers topped by pointed ogee roofs. Both back and front of the house are identical, save the carved swags and mouldings over the front door.

However, this is no mere façade, pinned onto an earlier house to conform with fashion – the House of Gray is genuine, through and through. The interior had finely proportioned rooms and 'extensive accommodation' when it was offered for sale in 1977. But ten years later there were no floors and very little roof, just a naked cinerous skeleton exposed to the rain. If Scottish houses often appear sombre it is the fault not of the design, but of the colour of the natural stone. The quarries of the north yield a depressing black rock without a hint of warmth. When varnished by the driving rain, the colour deepens to jet. If the House of Gray had been built in the Cotswolds it would have been heralded as one of the gems of our heritage. As it is, it has been almost forgotten, and now aptly illustrates its name; the dark hollow windows and a makeshift roof of black tar-paper amplify the funerary effect.

But once the rain has passed, the welcome heat of the afternoon sun washes a mottled radiance over the ashen stone, the shadows glowing like the blue of gunmetal. With relief, the stone absorbs the warmth and, gently, a light steam begins to rise – the moisture gathering in the shady hollows of the long grass, spores of mist in the chilly air as another day draws to a close.

Staircase towers, House of Gray

A bleak façade of rough-hewn granite, Wardhouse

WARDHOUSE

Aberdeenshire   Category B

To the north, in the hills of Aberdeenshire, the sun did not come out and shine on the remains of Wardhouse while I was there. In the cold light of a drizzly day the bleak façade of rough-hewn granite stood black among the sapling trees.

Wardhouse occupies a majestic but exposed site on the high slopes above the head waters of the river Urie, looking across to the distant Grampians. All around, the rolling agricultural land is giving way to the spread of sitka spruce and lodgepole pine descending from the higher slopes. Further up, the hill-tops are already capped in dark blankets of conifer plantation, now highlighted with a powdering of snow. In this black world the silhouette of Wardhouse is almost invisible, its wet stone blending subtly into the dark woods that stand behind it.

With a strong pediment above a clumsy Palladian façade, the design of Wardhouse is architecturally similar to the House of Gray, but it is not the work of such an expert hand. The stone is rough and the details are harsh, combining to lend it a cold demeanour. The gloom of this severe neo-Classicism in its severe landscape is exaggerated by the impersonal lack of evidence of the former estate. At both Belladrum in Inverness and Fotheringham in Fife, the house had been completely destroyed, but the estates live on; here, however, the wretched house remains alone, the sole reminder of a once-flourishing estate.

Up until the Second World War the house belonged to the Gordons of Jerez, famous for their sherry. During the War the Gordons were abroad looking after their interests in Spain, and Wardhouse was neglected. By 1945 they could no longer sustain the estate, and it was sold to a local firm who removed anything of value from it; it was again sold in 1953, but as was so often the case in Scotland, in order to avoid paying rates they unroofed the house, leaving it as a wreck. The whole estate was sold off in parcels, and the house was left to crumble. Once it had elaborate interiors and a jolly garden, but without a roof or anyone to look after the garden, it soon reverted to nature.

As the Forestry Commission gradually take over the policies, so the house sinks into the rising forest, and will probably not be discovered until the trees reach maturity and are felled some time during the next century.

A sign of the times, Wardhouse

Fragments of delicate plasterwork sticking to the wattles, Baron Hill

BARON HILL

Anglesey   Grade II

Above the seaside village of Beaumaris, on the Isle of Anglesey, stands the overgrown shell of Baron Hill. Home to generations of the Bulkeley family, the house was rebuilt in the style of Charles Barry in 1830, requisitioned during the Second World War, and now stands wrecked as a result. For many reasons, troops billeted in large country houses have so often been their last inhabitants. It seems strange that carelessness, envy or bad supervision has been responsible for irreparable damage to so many great houses, and it is sad that such damage was never compensated after the War; such are the feelings of the owners of these houses today.

At Baron Hill the troops overflowed into rows of Nissen huts in the gardens, and at some point someone lit a fire in a ventilation shaft and the roof caught fire. After the war the lead was removed from the damaged roof and soon the floors collapsed. Although the fire damage may not have been too severe, at the time the family were unable to repair it and when they came to be allowed back into the house its condition had already deteriorated rapidly.

Thus the shell stands forlornly looking out over the Menai Straits southwards to Snowdon – a view of unparalleled magnificence that now takes a bow as the final curtain of trees rises up from the terraces below. The once formal gardens are overgrown with saplings and peppered with the foundations of the Nissen huts. The Victorian topiary has exploded in starbursts of yew, only brambles and nettles climb the elegant steps from the lawn, and ancient cedars try in vain to shelter the hollow windows with their sparse limbs. The kitchen garden, once segmented by walls, greenhouses and water channels, is now a riot of weeds, although the occasional elegant iron framework is still visible.

Of the interior of the house, little remains. Fragments of delicate plasterwork still stick to the wattle and the fine eliptical stair hall is open to the sky. Four columns lean drunkenly against the walls, their job now done. The portico bears the autographs of local vandals who used to smash up whatever the army had left. Now, however, the gamekeeper dissuades them and other visitors from spending too much time at Baron Hill, with an admonishing finger poised at the ready on the trigger of his shotgun.

A riot of weeds in the greenhouses, Baron Hill

The portico bearing the autographs of local vandals, Baron Hill

The overgrown shell of Baron Hill

A glimpse of the house through the gates, Yeaton Pevery

YEATON PEVERY

Shropshire   Grade II*

Yeaton Pevery, now one hundred years old, has earned little of the respect due to a centenarian. The descendants of Sir Offley Wakeman, who built the house in 1891, have lived nearby in a modern house since the War, and have vigorously protected their isolation while the house has been left to rot.

Built to the designs of Sir Ashton Webb, Yeaton Pevery presents a powerful silhouette of strong red sandstone from across the fields near Shrewsbury. It was described by Pevsner as 'an astonishing Jacobean fantasy', and I was particularly attracted to its asymmetrical and lively design. The house, despite having been a school until the early 1970s, was reported to be in excellent order featuring surprisingly unaltered examples of Victorian interiors.

Having been excited by the interior of Woodchester Park, I was keen to paint these empty Victorian rooms. But initial enquiries in the area revealed that the owners would indeed protect their isolation and that I would find it difficult to see; certainly permission would have to be obtained to get *to* the house, let alone *into* it. A telephone call resulted in astonishment; "why on earth would an artist want to paint this house – it is all closed up and now badly vandalised, and anyway it's hideous" – this coupled with a flat refusal. Evidently Marcus Binney had experienced a similar rebuff, as he describes in the introduction. Suddenly I saw how one person's opinion, whether justified or not, could lead to the destruction of a house, even one listed as Grade II*. It was easier to understand now why so many houses had been torn down since the turn of the century, and all the more unforgivable that it could still happen today.

Aware of the dangers of trespass on the property of others, I had previously ventured along a path, marked on the Ordnance Survey map as a red dotted line that signifies a right of way; this path passes within a few hundred yards of the house, and from that distance it had certainly seemed to be in good condition without any evidence of the reported vandalism. When I strayed a few yards from the path, an estate employee sprang from nowhere to ensure that I was unable to have a closer look. With such vigilant protection, I wondered later *who* had actually been the vandals, so far from the town.

The stone tympanum over the front door, Yeaton Pevery

Shafts of sunlight through fragments of stained glass, Crawford Priory

CRAWFORD PRIORY

Fife   Category B

Crawford Priory is a good example of the baronial hall so popular in Victorian times. The earliest part dates from 1783, but as was the fashion it was completely rebuilt in 1813 to the order of Lady Mary Lindsay Crawford. It was again enlarged and altered in 1871, and the interior was refurbished by Lord Cochrane, her grandson, in 1920, when he installed much fine oak panelling.

Although perhaps not a very beautiful building, Crawford Priory was always richly maintained, that is until recently. The family were driven out in the 1960s by rising costs and the spread of dry-rot, and the furniture was removed, the shutters closed and the house was just left to quietly deteriorate unseen.

At the back of the house a tower has collapsed and much of the roof has fallen in, rendering the remainder of the house unsafe. The wind and rain have claimed the principal rooms, the fine plasterwork smashed, the oak panelling rotten and, in the great Gothic hall a superb fan-vaulted ceiling has been pulverized by falling masonry. Much of the stained glass remains, hanging in the lead-work or clinging to its hinges. Very soon this too will crash down into the mud and guano on the parquet flooring of the drawing room and hall.

In one of the bedrooms, there were once some beautiful handpainted wallpapers, depicting scenes from the adventures of Psyche. These had been copied exactly from the Château de Valençay, the 'Chambre du Roi' of which was decorated in Empire style for Talleyrand. The fate of these wall paintings is uncertain – surely they were rescued, or do they still cling to the damp walls, upstairs and out of reach, awaiting imminent and inevitable destruction?

In the gardens, the former terraces have sprouted young trees and the stone pillars and ornaments are either overgrown or have been smashed. Once the gardens were tended by a team of 20 gardeners, supervised by a head gardener smartly dressed in morning coat and spats, but their fine work is now indiscernible beneath the profusion of brambles and saplings. The grounds now provide a home for the pheasants, reared nearby for the estate shoot, and deer still wander gingerly about. Set into a wall in the courtyard there is a plaque that remembers one in particular:

AT THE PRIORY
Died at seven years old, the favourite Roe deer of GEORGE EARL of CRAWFURD, and LINDSAY, whom he daily fed, who followed him home and slept at his feet.

Placed here by LADY MARY L. CRAWFURD 1812

A Regency villa, Summerfold

SUMMERFOLD HOUSE

Surrey

Although Highcliffe Castle was the first house I painted in this series, it was not the first silent house I had experienced. As adventurous teenagers, a friend and I used to dare each other to go up to Summerfold House, on the top of a high hill not a half-mile from home.

The shell of the house evidently had been an adventure playground for many local kids – not just the usual graffiti-daubing vandals. One young romantic invited his lady out to dinner, and they walked in the moonlight up to Summerfold. There he had arranged a candle-lit picnic dinner for them in the rubble of the dining room – in black tie! History does not relate whether that relationship flourished as a result, but Summerfold certainly featured in the background of many a young heart.

It was as a shooting lodge that Summerfold was built for the Duke of Sutherland at the turn of this century. It is a compact Regency villa with the most superb view from the top of the Surrey Hills to Chanctonbury on the South Downs. On a clear winter's morning one could even see the distant shimmer of the sea through Shoreham Gap. The Duke was rarely in residence, but the house was made available to his friends who took advantage of its proximity to London, the most notable houseguests being Edward and Mrs Simpson.

At the outbreak of the War, Summerfold was enlisted as a lookout post and radio base, and saw active service while the Battle of Britain raged overhead. The Canadian troops manning the watch from the roof had a shock when an errant buzz-bomb crashed nearby, but the house was not damaged. After the War a radio listening post was maintained in the attic right up until the 1960s, by which time the rest of the house was falling down, and eventually it was abandoned.

As property prices in the Home Counties soared during the 1980s, Summerfold soon attracted attention. It was taken on by a young couple who used whatever spare time and funds they could muster on the Herculean task of restoring the house. Working from room to room, they gradually expanded their living quarters until, ten years later, it was finished. The wild garden was tamed and replanted, and in 1987 the view was greatly widened by the hand of the Almighty. Now one can stand on the terrace and perhaps see an artist sketching in his garden down below!

The garden façade from the terrace, Summerfold

SOURCES AND FURTHER READING

Aberpergwm House
   The Greater Houses Inv. of Anc. Monuments in Glamorgan.
      Vol. IV Part 1. HMSO.
   NMR-Wales surveys and reports.

Aberglasney
   Country Walk John Dyer 1726.
   NMR-Wales surveys and reports.

Ashmans Hall
   Burke's and Saville's Guide to Country Houses Vol. III 1981.
   Country Life, Oct. 1987.
   RCHM report.

Buchanan Castle
   My Ditty Box The Duke of Montrose. Jonathan Cape, 1952.

Buntingsdale Hall
   Country Life, May 1986.
   Country Life Vol. XLII, Nov. 1917.
   Burke's and Saville's Guide to Country Houses Vol. II.
   Our Vanishing Heritage Marcus Binney. Arlington Books.
   The Buildings of England, Shropshire Pevsner.

Cams Hall
   Hampshire Buildings Preservation Trust
      annual report, 1989.

Caradoc Court
   Burke's and Saville's Guide to Country Houses Vol. II.
   The Buildings of England, Herefordshire Pevsner.
   RCHM Vol. I.
   The Hereford Times (reports), 1977–88.

Copped Hall
   Country Life Vol. XXVII.
   Our Vanishing Heritage Marcus Binney. Arlington Books.
   Copped Hall, A Short Story. Raymond Cassidy.
      Waltham Abbey History Society, 1983.

Ecclesgrieg House
   123 Views of Royal Deeside Aberdeen Daily Journal.

Ecton Hall
   Country Life Vol. CXV.
   Our Vanishing Heritage Marcus Binney. Arlington Books.

Edwinsford House
   NMR-Wales survey and reports.

Gibside
   Landscape, Dec. 1987.
   Country Life Vols. LXXXVII; CXI; CLIV; CLVI.
   The Unhappy Countess Ralph Arnold. Constable, 1957.
   John Bowes and the Bowes Museum Charles E. Hardy.
      Frank Graham 1970.

Guy's Cliffe
   Country Life Vols. I; VII.
   Burke's and Saville's Guide to Country Houses Vol. II.
   A Short History of Guy's Cliffe G. C. Masonic Rooms Ltd.
      A. F. Porter, 1989.

Gwylfa Hiraethog
   Country Quest April 1963. Lord Devonport.

Highcliffe Castle
   Country Life, 22nd May 1986.
   Country Life Vols. XCI; CXXXIX; CXLII.
   Country Life Vol. LXX. (gardens)
   Transactions of the Ancient Monuments Society, 1968.

High Head Castle
   Country Life, 15th Oct. 1921.
   The Destruction of the Country House. Thames and
      Hudson, 1974.

House of Gray
   Sale particulars Oct. 1977.

Kirklinton Hall
  The Buildings of England, Cumberland Pevsner.

Loudon Castle
  Carrick Days D. C. Cuthbertson. Grant and Murray.
  History of Ayrshire James Shaw. Oliver & Boyd, 1953.

Mavisbank House
  The Independent, 2nd May 1989.
  The Classical County House in Scotland 1660–1800
    James Macauley. Faber and Faber 1987.
  Sir John Clerk Letters. S.R.O. File No. GD 18/4.

Melton Constable Hall
  Country Life, 16th Jan. 1986.
  Country Life Vols. XVIII; LXIV; LXXX; CLIV.
  The Field, 28th June 1986.

Minto House
  Famous Scottish Houses.

Oulton Hall
  The Buildings of England, Yorkshire Pevsner.

Pell Wall Hall
  Burke's and Saville's Guide to Country Houses Vol. II.
  Country Life Vol. CXIV.
  Country Life, 22nd Nov. 1984.
  Our Vanishing Heritage Marcus Binney. Arlington Books.
  Transactions of the Ancient Monuments Society, 1985.
  The Works of Sir John Soane Dorothy Stroud.
  World in Action Granada TV, 12th May 1986.
  The Times, 11th Jan. 1988.

Penicuik House
  The Castles and Mansions of the Lothians John Small.
    William Patterson, 1883.
  Edinburgh Tatler July 1968.
  Country Life Alistair Rowan, 15th and 22nd Aug. 1968.
  The Scottish Field Sheila Forman, 1953.
  The Classical Country House in Scotland 1660–1800
    James Macauley. Faber and Faber, 1987.

Piercefield House
  NMR-Wales surveys and reports.
  The Works of Sir John Soane Dorothy Stroud.

Revesby Abbey
  Country Life, 14th Jan. 1988.
  Sale particulars Aug. 1983.

Ruperra Castle
  The Greater Houses Inv. of Ancient Monuments in
    Glamorgan Vol. IV Part 1. HMSO.
  Glamorgan – Its History & Topography C. J. O. Evans.
    William Lewis, 1938.
  Historic Architecture of Wales J. B. Hilling.
  Ruperra Castle Tony Friend. Newport Local History
    Society, 1984.

Sinai Park
  Staffordshire County Council Architectural and
    Buildings Survey.

Stocken Hall
  Our Vanishing Heritage Marcus Binney. Arlington Books.

Urie House
  123 Views of Royal Deeside Aberdeen Daily Journal.

Vale Royal Abbey
  Cheshire County Council survey and reports.
  The Buildings of England, Cheshire Pevsner.

Witley Court
  Country Life Vols. II; XCVII; XCVIII; CXI.
  Country Life Vol. CXLIII (gardens).
  The Buildings of England, Worcestershire Pevsner

Woodchester Park
  Landscape, April 1988.
  Country Life Vol. CXLV, 6th Feb. 1969.
  The Victorian Country House M. Girouard, 1979.
  RCHM report.
  Woodchester Mansion Trust Guide Duff Hart-Davis.

Yeaton Pevery
  Burke's and Saville's Guide to Country Houses Vol. II.
  The Buildings of England, Shropshire Pevsner.

In addition, much information on most of the houses is
contained in the following publications by 'SAVE Britain's
Heritage':
  Endangered Domains Julia Woolton, 1985.
  The Country House – To Be or Not to Be Marcus Binney
    and Kit Martin, 1982.
  The Lost Houses of Scotland 1980.
  The Lost Houses of Wales Thomas Lloyd, 1986.
  House at Risk in Ayrshire, 1989.
  Scotland's Endangered Houses Marcus Dean and Mary
    Miers, 1990.

LIST OF ILLUSTRATIONS

Page   Size

  2   Virginia creeper almost obscuring the façade of Edwinsford House   22″×15″

  7   The façade of the house was once used for target practice, Piercefield   14″×10″

  8   The garden gates swung open, Caradoc Court   detail

  9   Looking into the stair hall, Oulton Park   detail

10   Three storeys of stairs, Cams Hall   detail

11   A stone fountain, Caradoc Court   8″×6″

12   The stairs at Urie House – a colour note   14″×10″

13   The house completely hidden in the trees, Pell Wall Hall   detail

14   Vast in conception and extravagant in execution, Witley Court   21″×11″

15   The drawing room fireplace, Ecton Hall – a colour note   8″×6″

16   Broken window and shutters ajar, Stocken Hall   15″×11″

17   Foul graffiti cover the walls, Dunmore House   detail

18   The bridge at Edwinsford – a colour note   12″×10″

19   An elegant retreat for a man of affairs, Mavisbank House   detail

20   The broken front door, Aberpergwm   8″×6″

21   A fan-vaulted ceiling pulverised by falling masonry, Crawford Priory   14″×10″

22   A carved marble doorcase from France at Highcliffe   22″×15″

24   Under the great *porte-cochère*, Highcliffe   30″×22″

25   On a summer's afternoon, Highcliffe   15″×11″

26   At the foot of the staircase, Ashmans Hall   18″×14″

27   Cow parsley at Ashmans Hall   11″×10″

28   The white brick Regency façade of Ashmans Hall   14″×10″

29   The Imperial staircase of cantilevered stone, Ashmans Hall   30″×22″

30   A large part of the façade cascaded into the valley, Minto House   15″×11″

31   A curved porch standing in the crook of a right-angle, Minto House   15″×11″

32   The drive lined with flowering fireweed, High Head Castle   15″×12″

33   Among the tall weeds on the steps, High Head Castle   16″×12″

34   The pavilion in the light of a full moon, Copped Hall   22″×15″

35   '*Me umbra regit . . .*', a sundial on the pediment, Copped Hall   14″×10″

36   A familiar landmark, the shell of Copped Hall   12″×9″

37	A pavilion at Copped Hall	30″×22″
38	Proud protruding towers and gables, Buchanan Castle	22″×15″
39	At the back of Buchanan Castle	15″×11″
40	Collapsed gables and empty mullions against the sky, Caradoc	30″×22″
41	The Victorian neo-Jacobean façade, Caradoc	12″×9″
42	The timber-framed 16th-century house, Caradoc	14″×10″
43	The garden gates swung open, Caradoc	22″×15″
44	The owner's caravan in front of Kirklinton	22″×15″
45	The guardians of Kirklinton	14″×10″
46	A gaunt silhouette from across the river, Guy's Cliffe	22″×15″
47	The back door and courtyard, Guy's Cliffe	14″×10″
48	The principal door, Guy's Cliffe – a colour note	15″×11″
49	The stairs at Guy's Cliffe	15″×11″
50	Above the mud of rotten wood, foul graffiti cover the walls of Dunmore	22″×15″
51	Ivy covering the *porte-cochère*, Dunmore	16″×12″
52	A giant portico and curved wing leading to the orangery, Witley Court	36″×18″
53	The steps to the main door, Witley Court	14″×10″
54	The Poseidon Fountain, 20 tons of sculpted stone, Witley Court	22″×15″
55	The steps from the courtyard, Witley Court	16″×12″
56	Aberglasney disintergrates in its damp gloomy valley	15″×11″
58	*'Keep ye gods this humble seat, For ever pleasant, private, neat'*, Aberglasney	14″×10″
59	A fine two-storeyed hall full of junk, Aberglasney	15″×11″
60	The river was a swollen torrent under the old bridge, Edwinsford	30″×22″
61	An important gentry-house, Edwinsford	14″×10″
62	The ornamental canal and Georgian façade, Stocken Hall	22″×15″
63	A long finger of sunlight in the drawing room, Stocken Hall	15″×11″
64	Looking into the stair hall at Oulton	22″×15″
65	Crisp stonework on the portico of Oulton Hall	15″×11″
66	Rich strap work on the porch, Revesby	22″×11″
68	A detail of carving in the library, Revesby	15″×11″
69	A dusty silence in the principal rooms, Revesby	30″×22″
70	A shroud of ivy obliterating the façade of Poltalloch	22″×15″
71	New Poltalloch from the fields	15″×11″
72	The black stones of Old Poltalloch	16″×12″
73	The rich stone splashed with lichen, Poltalloch	22″×15″
74	The drawing room fireplace rises above a heap of plaster, Ecton	30″×22″
75	The pastoral Northamptonshire countryside around Ecton Hall	15″×11″
76	An elegant retreat for a man of affairs, Mavisbank	30″×22″
78	The ruined façade of Mavisbank – a drawing	15″×11″

79	Mavisbank – a colour note	12″×9″
80	The walls still standing, Penicuik	22″×15″
81	A substantial Neo-Classical mansion, Penicuik	12″×10″
82	Mottled light on the drive, Penicuik	14″×10″
83	The broken balustrade in the portico, Penicuik	22″×15″
84	The house hidden in the trees, Pell Wall	30″×22″
85	The twisted balustrade, Pell Wall	12″×9″
86	The façade cleared of trees, Pell Wall	14″×10″
87	Marble columns in a snowy landscape, Pell Wall	22″×15″
88	The hall and saloon at Piercefield	30″×22″
89	A Classical pavilion flanking the house, Piercefield	12″×9″
90	The portico at Bettisfield in the late afternoon	15″×11″
91	A dusty mirror and over-mantle in the hall, Bettisfield	15″×11″
92	Sun through the windows of the Green Drawing Room, Bettisfield	22″×15″
93	Greek-Revival plasterwork and swagged friezes, Bettisfield	22″×15″
94	The splintered remains of a 17th-century staircase, Bank Hall	30″×22″
96	Bank Hall looming in the flurries of a snowstorm	22″×15″
97	The greenhouse full of brambles, Bank Hall	14″×10″
98	'The Watch–Tower of the Mountain', Gwylfa Hiraethog	22″×15″
99	Driven snow and wet granite, Gwylfa Hiraethog	15″×11″
100	Melton Constable	12″×10″
101	A dried-up fountain on the front lawn, Melton Constable	18″×14″
102	A stained-glass window diffusing light onto dusty treads, Ecclesgrieg	15″×11″
103	The Victorian garden with its balustrades and parterres, Ecclesgrieg	14″×10″
104	The drive, no more than tractor tracks through a field, Urie House	15″×11″
105	A flight of steps hidden in the garden, Urie House	11″×9″
106	Stone stairs at Urie House that lead nowhere	22″×15″
107	A spectacular ruined shell visible from afar, Urie House	12″×9″
108	The overgrown terraces of the Italian garden at Belladrum	22″×15″
109	Lupins run wild at Belladrum	14″×10″
110	The 1200-year-old 'Yew of Loudon'	15″×11″
111	'The Windsor of Scotland', Loudon Castle	14″×10″
112	The Great Hall with its brace and hammer-beam roof, Vale Royal Abbey	22″×15″
113	The rambling structure of Vale Royal Abbey	14″×10″
114	Ash trees in the Great Banqueting Hall, Ruperra	30″×22″
115	The royal coat of arms, Ruperra – a sketch	7″×5″
116	One of the towers split from top to bottom, Ruperra	14′×10″
117	The royal coat of arms above the south porch of Ruperra	15″×11″
118	Salmon-pink brickwork and whitewash, Pickhill	15″×11″

119 The open door and rubble within, Pickhill   14″×10″

120 Weeds and flowers on the front steps, Buntingsdale   22″×15″

121 The lantern on the steps, Buntingsdale   14″×10″

122 Three storeys of precise brickwork and carved stone pilasters, Buntingsdale   14″×10″

123 The door to the entrance hall, Buntingsdale   15″×11″

124 *'There was a crooked man who had a crooked house'*, Sinai Park   22″×15″

126 A pair of wrought-iron gates hanging drunkenly from the gateposts, Aberpergwm   22″×15″

127 The front door at Aberpergwm   15″×11″

128 Stone fireplaces at Woodchester   22″×15″

130 The house and chapel windows from the east, Woodchester   14″×10″

131 The windows unglazed and the walls unplastered, Woodchester   16″×12″

132 Sunlight through the mullion windows, Gibside   22″×15″

133 A detail of the coat of arms over the front door, Gibside   5″×7″

134 Three storeys of stairs, Cams Hall   30″×22″

136 A framework of scaffolding around Cams Hall   14″×10″

137 Fragments of marble column and plaster cornice, Cams Hall   16″×12″

138 A mottled radiance over the ashen stone of House of Gray   15″×11″

139 Staircase towers, House of Gray   14″×10″

140 A bleak façade of rough-hewn granite, Wardhouse   15″×11″

141 A sign of the times, Wardhouse   14″×10″

142 Fragments of delicate plasterwork sticking to the wattles, Baron Hill   22″×15″

143 A riot of weeds in the greenhouses, Baron Hill   14″×10″

144 The portico bearing the autographs of local vandals, Baron Hill   22″×15″

145 The overgrown shell of Baron Hill   14″×10″

146 A glimpse of the house through the gates, Yeaton Pevery   22″×15″

147 The stone tympanum over the front door, Yeaton Pevery   15″×11″

148 Shafts of sunlight through fragments of stained glass, Crawford Priory   16″×12″

150 A Regency villa, Summerfold   22″×15″

151 The garden façade from the terrace, Summerfold   15″×11″

160 Endpiece, Baron Hill   15″×11″

INDEX

A

Abbey of Jumièges 23
Aberglasney 56–9
Aberpergwm House 20, 126–7
Adam, Robert 78, 111
Adam, William 78, 139
Ashmans Hall 26–9
Astley family 101

B

Baird, Alexander 105
Bank Hall 94–7
Banks, Sir Joseph 67
Barclay-Allardyce, Capt. R. 105
Barclays of Urie 105
Barlaston Hall 13
Baron Hill 142–5, 160
Barrington Court 18
Barry, Charles 143
Belladrum House 108–9
Benham Park 18
Bettisfield Park 90–3
Binney, Marcus 13, 15–20, 147
Blayds, John 65
Bonomi, Joseph 89
Bowes, John 133
Bowes, Mary Eleanor 133
Bowes, Sir George 133
British Historic Buildings Trust 85
Brougham, Henry Richmond 33
Brown, Capability 18, 39, 89
Buchanan Castle 38–9
Bucknall, Benjamin 129
Bulkeley family 143
Buntingsdale Hall 19, 120–3
Burn, William 67, 72

C

Campbell clan 71
Cams Hall 10, 134–7
Caradoc Court 8, 11, 40–3
Carnac, General 135

Charles I 115
Château de Valançay 149
Cholmondeley family 113
Cistercian abbey 113
Clay, Henry Hastings 89
Clerk, James 81
Clerk, Sir John of Penicuik 77
Cochrane, Lord 149
Conyers, Edward 35
Copped Hall 34–7
Country House, historical role of 11
Country Life 33, 36, 75
Crawford, Lady Mary Lindsay 149
Crawford Priory 20, 148–9
Crowcombe Court 16
Cullen 16, 18

D

Danson Hill 16
Dawkes, Samuel 53
Delmé, John 135
'Destruction of the Country House', The
   Exhibition of 13, 15
Devonport, Lord 99
Digby family 41
Donthorne, W. 23
Dudley, earls of 52–3
Dunmore House 17, 50–1
Dyer, John 57

E

Ecclesgrieg House 102–3
Ecton Hall 15, 74–5
Edward I 113
Edward VI 35
Edward VII 54
Edwinsford House 2, 60–1
Elizabeth I 35
Elliot, Archibald 111
English Heritage 18

F

Foley, Lord 53
Fountains, at Witley Court 53
Fraser, Colonel James 109
Fraser clan 109
Freemasons 48

G

Gibbons, Grinling 101
Gibbs, style of 33
Gibside 132–3
Gordons of Jerez 141
Grand Tour 81
Gray, Lord 139
Greatheed, Bertie 47
Guy's Cliffe 46–9
Gwylfa Hiraethog 98–9

H

Hamilton, Emma 135
Hanmer, Lord 91
Harris, John 13
Harrowes, Dr 78
Heneage, Thomas 35
Henry VIII 113, 125
Heywood, Lt. Col. George 41
Highcliffe Castle 16, 23–5
High Head Castle 32–3
Hills, Major John 33
Holcroft, Thomas 113
House of Gray 138–9
Hylands 16

J

Jones, Inigo 115

K

Kaiser Wilhelm 23
Kirklinton Hall 44–5

L

Lancaster, Osbert 15

Landmark Trust 16, 51
Leith, William 129
Leroux, Jacob 135
Lilford, Lord 95
Llangoed Castle 18
Losey, Joseph 101
Lothian Building Preservation Trust 78
Loudon Castle 110–11
Loudon, Countess of 111
Lyon, John, Earl of Strathmore 133

M

MacDonald clan 71
Mackworth, Bulkeley 121
Malcolms of Duntrune 71
Mary Tudor 35
Mavisbank House 19, 77–9
Melton Constable 20, 100–1
Merry, Ian 109
Merry, James 109
Midsummer Night's Dream, A 35
Minto, Earl of 31
Minto House 30–1
Montrose, dukes of 39
Morgan, Courtney 115
Morgan, Sir Thomas 115

N

National Trust for Scotland 51
Niven, Ninian 109
Northumberland, dukes of 47

O

Oulton Hall 9, 64–5

P

Paget, Sir William 125
Paine, James 133
Pell Wall Hall 84–7
Penicuik House 80–3
Percy, Lord Algernon 47

Pickhill Hall 118–19
Piercefield House 6, 88–9
Pineapple folly 51
Poltalloch House 70–3
Portwood, George 63
Pratt, Sir Roger 101

R

Rede, Robert 27
Repton, Humphrey 65
Revesby Abbey 18, 66–9
Robinson family 27
Royal family, and Highcliffe Castle 23
Rudd, Bishop Anthony 57
Ruperra Castle 114–17

S

Sanderson, John 35
SAVE Britain's Heritage 13, 15
Scout Hall 16
Scudamore, Viscounts 41
Simpson, Mrs 151
Sinai Park 124–5
Smirke, Robert 65
Smirke, Sydney 65
Smith, Francis 119, 121
Smith, George 89
Smith, Sir Herbert 54
Smith, Sir John 16
Smythson, Robert 115
Soane, Sir John 85, 89
Sotheby, Lady 75
Stanhope, J. Banks 67
Stevenson, Mr 78
Stocken Hall 16, 62–3
Stoney, Captain 133
Strathmore, Earl of 133
Strong, Roy 13
Stuart, James 109
Stuart, Lord Charles de Rothesay 23
Summerfold House 150–1
Sutherland, Duke of 151

T

Treaty of Union, 1705 111
Tredegar, Viscount 115
Trubshaw, Richard 119

U

Urie House 12, 104–7

V

Vale Royal Abbey 112–13
Veronese frescos 91
Victoria and Albert museum exhibition 13, 15
Viollet-le-Duc, Eugène 129
Viscounts Dudley 53

W

Wakeman, Sir Offley 147
Ward, Lord William 53
Wardhouse 140–1
Warwick, Guy of 47
Webb, Sir Ashton 147
Webster, George 95
Westminster, Duke of 101
Wilkins, William 51
Williams family 127
Williams-Ellis, Sir Clough 18
Windsor, Duke of 151
Witley Court 14, 52–5
Wood, Lt. Col. Mark 89
Woodchester Park 128–131
Wren, Sir Christopher 101
Wyatt, James 91
Wythes, George 36

Y

Yeaton Pevery 146–7
Yew of Loudon 110–11

Z

Zelotti frescos 91

"In my beginning is my end. In succession
Houses rise and fall, crumble, are extended,
Are removed, destroyed, restored, or in their place
Is an open field, or a factory, or a by-pass.
Old stone to new building, old timber to new fires,
Old fires to ashes, and ashes to the earth. . ."

T. S. Eliot
'East Coker'